Soulprints

The Ray S. Anderson Collection

Ray Sherman Anderson (1925–2009) worked the soil and tended the animals of a South Dakota farm, planted and pastored a church in Southern California, and completed a PhD degree in theology with Thomas F. Torrance in New College Edinburgh. He began his professional teaching career at Westmont College, and then taught and served in various administrative capacities at Fuller Theological Seminary for thirty-three years (retiring as Professor Emeritus of Theology and Ministry). While teaching at Fuller, he served as a parish pastor, always insisting that theology and ministry go hand-in-hand.

The pastoral theologian who began his teaching career in middle age penned twenty-seven books. Like Karl Barth, Prof. Anderson articulated a theology of and for the church based on God's own ministry of revelation and reconciliation in the world. As professor and pastor, he modeled an incarnational, evangelical passion for the healing of humanity by Jesus Christ, who is *both* God's self-revelation to us *and* the reconciliation of our broken humanity to the triune God. His gift of relating suffering and alienated humans to Christ existing as community (Dietrich Bonhoeffer) is a recurrent motif throughout his life, ministry, and works.

The Ray S. Anderson Collection comprises books by Ray Anderson, an introductory text to his theology by Christian D. Kettler, two edited volumes that celebrate his distinguished academic career (*Incarnational Ministry: The Presence of Christ in Church, Society, and Family* and *On Being Christian . . . and Human*), and a reprint of an Edification volume that focuses on Ray Anderson's contributions to the field of Christian Psychology. A word of gratitude is due to The Society of Christian Psychology and its parent organization, The American Association for Christian Counselors, for their permission to make the *Edification* issue available in book form. Jim Tedrick of Wipf and Stock Publishers deserves a special word of thanks for publishing many of Ray Anderson's books and commissioning this collection of works to continue his legacy.

Todd H. Speidell, General Editor

Soulprints

Ray S. Anderson

Personal Reflections on
Faith, Hope and Love

WIPF & STOCK · Eugene, Oregon

Wipf and Stock Publishers
199 W 8th Ave, Suite 3
Eugene, OR 97401

Soulprints
By Anderson, Ray S. and Speidell, Todd H.
Copyright©1996 by Anderson, Ray S.
ISBN 13: 978-1-61097-133-1
Publication date 5/1/2011
Previously published by Fuller Seminary Press, 1996

Contents

Soulprints 1

Soulmates 2

Part One

Breaking Fresh Ground 1962-1970 5

Part Two

Wild Flowers and Wanton Words 95

Lara 97
Joshua Ray 99
Tondi 101
Brandon 103
Brogan 105
Nathan 107
Scott Andrew 109
Todd 111
To Eve, On Her Birthday 113
For Mary 114
A Stone for My Hand 117
Yet Not My Will 118

I Could Weep   119
Incarnation   121
A Sense of Createdness   122
An Elegy for God   124
A Resurrection   125
Consecration   127
The Child   128
Annunciation at Advent   129
Haiku   130
Two Spirits   132
Thanks for Yesterday   133
My Reason   134
Thanks be to God   135
Bound to Give Thanks   136
Faces   137
Fragments of the Whole   139
Sundown in Sedona   141
A Prayer   144

Part Three

Pools of Reflection and Wonder   147

Epilogue

Judas Come Home, All is Forgiven   183

References   194

Soulprints

Soulprints, like fingerprints,
are unique to each person
    and invisible to the naked eye.
When dusted with the whisper of words,
soulprints, like fingerprints,
    can be transferred as images,
        leaving traces of the self
for others to discover
        if they wish.
This slice of my soul
is cut straight through the center.
If these pages are a pilgrimage,
it is not from then to now
        but from fear to faith
            from no to yes
            and from me to you !
This does not chronicle where I have been
        but where I am.
This is what it is to be me.
And reading this, to know me
        if you wish.
I own every doubt, every question
        and I am every paradox.
And I lie exposed and defenseless
        to the charge of incoherence
            and inconsistency
        from those who are afraid,
        of their own complexities.
But to you, who discover
that the vantage point is the same,
I am also defenseless, opened up
        to being trusted, understood--
            loved.

Soulmates

"The heart knows its own bitterness, and no stranger shares its joy."
Proverbs 14:10

It was a formidable thing
    Unassailable by the brazen stranger
        Impenetrable by the closest friend
    This great wall around my heart.
It is both ageless and contemporary.
Bright new stones set among mossy antiques.
    It has always been -- yet in constant construction.
It is difficult to determine its origin -
was the first stone mortared with prenatal loneliness?
    Or quickly laid with the first fearful awareness of others?
    To those outside -- it is an offense and a threat.
    They plaster its uneven surface with stinging labels

"independent --

    proud --

        cold -- - "
But I am aware--I read their distorted posters and watch them
    with curious detachment.
For the wall is strangely built.
    Opaque to those without--
      but transparently clear in its view from within.
Strange--the thicker it is built, the clearer it becomes.
There are times when the lucid insight becomes unbearable--
    but the smooth inner walls will hold no covering--
        nor will they be darkened.
    I covet their blindness--yet cherish my vision.
        I am alone--but not idle.
        I am silent--but not empty.

There is much to do.
The lamp of awareness is an insatiable torch--
    as quickly as the reality of one moment is grasped,
    the light reveals another to be discovered --
        interpreted--
            savored.
With ubiquitous haste I search the illimitable depths of life,
distilling the sweet drops of the eternal from the waste of time.
    It becomes increasingly difficult to converse.
    The painful intimacy of family life has no vocabulary.
The casual talk of friends is a laborious and fatiguing pretense.
    The wall is a friend.
    I lean against it with sadness and am comforted by its
        strength.
    It has taken everything from me--there is nothing left
        but the individual.
    My loneliness is complete--
        I am a prisoner of my own awareness.
It was an imperceptible thing--
    impossible to see directly--only obliquely visible
There was a presence that was not myself.
But it was impossible! The wall was secure--
    no carelessness had left it in disrepair
    nor had unguarded moment opened its strength.
        Yet, it could not be denied
        there was a presence--
        not observed but observing...
        not without the wall--but within!
The view was as clear as for myself--both were viewing
the same world--from the same side of the transparent wall!
At first it was unbelievable --- then inescapable.
    It was enough to realize that the wall was still there
        yet there was a difference.
There were many things to do--
and it was difficult to remember there was no need of haste.

I proudly revealed the priceless jewels mined
    from a thousand moments of time--and kept
        for just such an impossible showing.

Often we simply leaned against the wall with
    wordless oneness
        viewing--
            sharing--
                experiencing.
The wall is transformed--
    what was once a prison has become a sanctuary.

The plant that now grows within this shelter is a fragile thing.
    So exquisite are its flowers that a brush of
        temporal air would wilt its
            imperishable petals . . .
    The fragrance of its perfume so delicate
        that the dust of words would choke it.

    The wall is a friend.

PART ONE

Breaking Fresh Ground: 1962-1970

He broke fresh ground--because, and only because, he had the courage to go ahead without asking whether others were following or even understood. He had no need for the divided responsibility in which others seek to be safe from ridicule, because he had been granted a faith which required no confirmation--a contact with reality, light and intense like the touch of a loved hand; a union in self-surrender without self-destruction, where his heart was lucid and his mind loving.

Dag Hammarskjold

MAY 28, 1962

I have often struggled with the urge to write. In each case it has seemed premature and ambiguous. Not that I have no thoughts--but they are embryos of ideas and feelings which produce stillborn progeny when pushed into the light.

Perhaps I fear that writing would become an intoxicating disease that left me no room or time for anything. The power of words and the possibilities of expression are so tremendous that I fairly burst with ecstasy--and yet my lips move so laboriously, and I curse the shallowness of a vocabulary purchased with the cheap coin of expediency in days of curious and desperate loneliness. I am chagrined at the length of time it has taken me to discover the reality of life in its most polyphonous form. It cannot be entirely attributed to the provincialism of the South Dakota plains, though heaven knows I carried that beyond the boundaries of even the most insecure self--image.

It is hard to say what has happened to me in the past few years. I know this--the decision to leave the farm and go to Seminary was still a part of the same compulsive search for a vocation which would satisfy my insatiable hunger for self fulfillment. I had no doubts that it might fail--nothing has ever failed me. I will not permit it. What cannot be accomplished by skill, I do through passion. The important thing is not the product but the triumph of self respect and the attainment of a personal goal. This is not to say that there was no spiritual dimension to my decision. There was more of a spiritual motive attributed to it by others than by myself I fear. I was under no illusions--even God's will came within the circumference of my own thought.

It is not hard to remember the attitude I had the first year in Seminary. The problem was simple. The world needed a Savior and I would go to the world with the solution. It did not occur to me that there was anything more complex than that. I conceived of my ministry as largely repetition. There was only one message and it was only a matter of repeating it with a few variations and with new illustrations. The extent of my ministry was unlimited--not because of the possibilities of relating the truth of Christ to the human situation, but because of the population of the world which would provide me with an inexhaustible audience. I finally had found a vocation sufficient to match my tremendous intensity.

Somewhere in the midst of this pathetic scene, there was a change.

It might have started with the books. The stimulating reading that was a part of a theological curriculum awakened a sleeping giant. Philosophy was a field assumed to belong to the repertoire of a pre--theological student. It was a stranger to me--an alien intruder into the world of corn, cows and cockleburs. I read--I probed--I questioned. Milking the accumulated wisdom of a dozen others. A few months was all that was needed to give me a working acquaintance with the premises of philosophy, from there I could walk alone. Literature was somehow associated in my mind with the drudgery of a thousand hours spent in hopeless English classes. With amazement I was introduced to the passion of life through the lives and words of others like myself.

And then of course, I was not without friends. They disarmed me with their love and captivated me by their genuineness. Not many, but a few. Enough. It doesn't take a multitude of friends, only one or two who create the dialectic of self revelation. There are many forces and many faces--it will take more than a few paragraphs to find them all. But then I have time.

I just had a call from a friend. It reminded me,

are these words written to be read or to be filed and forgotten? To be read, of course! It is foolish to think that they do not bear the same desperate need of recognition that clings to my own heart.

It is not this awareness that makes the writing difficult . . . it perhaps makes it easier. For somehow I feel that the painfulness of framing thoughts that stand exposed is not due so much to their revelation to a friend as to my own fearful self.

Why do I write? I do not know. Perhaps it is a therapy of desperation in an attempt to clear my mind of a thousand conflicting thoughts. Perhaps it is a search for reality amidst the fantasy of feeling and knowing.

I do know this: my life would be worthwhile and acceptable if only I could say something new and relevant. Only a hundred words would suffice if they were every one true, and original. It is not difficult to learn the smooth phrases that others have coined. It is not difficult to walk where others have worn a smooth path--or even where only one other has gone ahead. But to apply the uniqueness of one human spirit to the fantastic possibilities of life and create a paragraph of meaning--this is worthy of life itself. It will take time--

and the greater part of my life. The words will only come at the very end. In fact, they I cannot come before--if they did, what would come after? I live for these words. I am content that if my life is ended now, I have said them. If I live to speak again another week, I have not, and must strain to say them in every message.

It is time to leave--the day has been good. I feel better for having written these words. I trust they shall not be the last.

MAY 29, 1962

The new light of the morning brings possibility to meet expectation--life is a constant joy to me. I have been discouraged. There are times when I battle the weariness of maintaining balance and feel the pull of disintegration. Yet, I doubt that there has ever been a time in my life when I have felt more joy and hope than at this time.

I reflected this morning as I read a few pages from a scholarly and perceptive essay on the ethics of our modern business society--where is the limit of knowledge? On every side I see men who have given their lives to the pursuit of knowledge and have become experts in certain fields. Some men simply overwhelm me with their fantastic acquaintance with so many truths. Can one man know everything? Of course not. Then what should he know? How is he to choose out of all the possible knowledge in the world that which he shall possess?

One man can devote his life to the study of New Testament Greek and speak with authority in this field. I could do that. But I could do little else. And having done nothing else would I have more wisdom or less ? Or, I could refuse specialization--become a general practitioner of life so to speak. Would this be a dilution of potential? Would my spirit be so attenuated that effectiveness would be lost?

One thing I have noticed--every man has his distortion. No matter how erudite and skillful is his knowledge, he betrays himself at some point when portrayed against the horizon of reality. Bonhoeffer, for example, in his letters from prison reveals a tremendous capacity for objective re--evaluation of his own first premises. He is constantly going beyond his own thinking, which by the way, is one of the keys to his growth as far as I am concerned, and yet when it comes to the subject of Baptism, he emerges with distinct Lutheran presuppositions.

I think I fear distortion as much as anything. It is far too easy to become so accustomed to moving within the boundaries of one's own presuppositions that reality becomes identified with self concepts. I am not sure, but somehow I feel that the secret of wisdom (and maturity) lies in knowledge without distortion. This means one must move slowly, and constantly keep everything in relationship to reality.

The great idea: somehow everything relates to everything. The world has meaning and life is not senseless. This means that suffering as well as joy is part of the fabric. That from the perspective of the individual everything can be integrated into a relevant picture with constant check for reality.
. . . suffering as well as joy.

The presence of distortion is so subtle that I spend as much time tearing down as building. Maybe this is part of my present feeling. I am impatient to build -- -- -- I fear the edifice that I might build, for it may be a distortion.

So here I stand--surrounded with a thousand ideas, and helpless to build anything for fear of unreality.

--or is this building of a sort?

I am obsessed with this thought:

ONLY IN RELATIONSHIP IS THERE FREEDOM FROM DISTORTION.

I hope to do much with this thought.

MAY 31, 1962

I mean to say something today about relationship and distortion. But first there is something dangling from previous thoughts expressed in fragmentary form.

That is the difference between uniqueness and greatness. It strikes me that uniqueness is to be preferred to greatness. Kierkegaard was a great man. It is incontrovertible, and will manifest itself in yet greater ways through the next generation. However, and here I must qualify my feeling to guard it from presumption, I possess something that Kierkegaard did not have--the perspective of my own life. All that Kierkegaard was and said can be known by me and to that, I add my own perspective--I see him in relationship to reality. This was impossible for him. I need not add, that it is just as impossible for me to see myself in relationship to reality as it was for him, but then there remains the possibility of uniqueness for others!

I only mean to say this; the uniqueness of individuality is a great thought.

It is not a novel thought, yet it must be discovered by every person. It cannot be taught--only experienced. Yet it cannot be experienced without a teacher. Kierkegaard taught me to discover the uniqueness of my own self--and I promptly treasured my uniqueness more than his greatness.

He would not mind.

This is why I cannot settle for mere greatness and become a scholar. Professional dexterity in anyone of the multitudinous fields of human knowledge is far too limited in scope to satisfy the range of individual uniqueness. Let others forage in the dry dust of a career--I shall encompass their labors within the perspective of my own life and use their knowledge to build my wisdom.

Not that I am a parasite. I simply do not recognize the copyright of knowledge. What others have learned can be appropriated by me through the process of distillation and related to the great idea. I shall never know the secrets of the professional man--but neither will I spend a lifetime wandering in the labyrinth of ways that lead to one form of knowledge. I only need to know the relationship of that labyrinth to a hundred others--and this may turn out to be the more prodigious effort.

I promised myself an excursion into the depths of relationship in life.

It is a dimension in my present thinking that holds the most promise. The starting point is with the self itself. Efforts to define the self fail through the finitude of words and infinitude of thought. Kierkegaard stated it with the true sense of paradox:

"In the relation between two (soul and body), the relation is the third term as a negative unity, and the two relate themselves to the relation, and in the relation to the relation . . . if on the contrary the relation relates itself to its own self, the relation is then the positive third term, and this is the self. Such a derived, constituted, relation is the human self, a relation which relates itself to its own self, and in relating itself to its own self relates itself to another . . .By relating itself to its own self and by willing to be itself, the self is grounded transparently in the Power which constituted it."

I think I understand this--tomorrow I shall discover whether I do or not!

> The sun
> > is breaking
> > > out of the clouds

I think it will be a good day.

JUNE 3, 1962

"The act of love is, like the act of faith, a surrender; and I believe that the one conditions the other . . . I cannot regret that I loved her, because love is independent of its expression--and it was only my expression of it. that was contrary to the moral law. This I regret and have confessed and prayed to be forgiven . . . But even in sin, the act of love --done with love--is shadowed with divinity. Its conformity may be at fault, but its nature is not altered, and its nature is creative, communicative, splendid in surrender . . . "

Her reasoning is poetic--but not altogether without foundation. The essence of personal relationship is communication of spirit and this does transcend its own expression, but it is not independent of it. The distinction is important. To create the hiatus between the reality of love and its expression in order to preserve love from the consequences of its inappropriate expression gives up too much to gain too little. To make the spirit independent of its temporal expression severs temporal reality from its close affinity with the reality of the eternal. Man is both dust and spirit and is not independent of his own nature.

The moral law is not the arbitration of the

expression in time but the context of the spirit in eternity. When the spirit communicates without the possibility of temporal expression there *is* reality but not without suffering. And the suffering is just this: the spirit has discovered possibilities which have no appropriate expression in time (not due to the moral law of time, but the integrity of the eternal).

Nevertheless, time is a friend -- there are no possibilities in eternity because there is no contingency. The spirit's confinement within the horizons of time is not a prison but the very essence of personhood. Heaven only has meaning because life has been *lived* first. The heart is able to endure the suffering of time because it is content with having been discovered in time in order that it may be fulfilled in eternity. Not to have been discovered is a greater threat than the suffering of the spirit in its limitation by the temporal.

Even the poet cannot have both temporal expression and eternal reality without destroying the meaning of both.

Hence the dialectic ---- faith and resignation.

I bow before the truth and beauty of this phrase ". . . even in sin, the act of love--done with love--is shadowed with divinity."

JUNE 5, 1962

"Hope deferred makes the heart sick . . ."
Proverbs 13:12a

The heart has little patience with the rules of temporal life--yet its sickness is not impatience but hope. That which in time is called a virtue (patience) in the eternal becomes suffering. That the two exist simultaneously is no surprise to the heart which fears nothing so much as impatience (sin) and immediacy (despair).

It cannot be denied that the temporal forges chains which the eternal cannot shake off without betraying its own integrity. The weight of these chains is a burden--their sharp edges irritating--their limits confining. It is the joy of faith to discern the difference between the anticipated freedom from the chains (temporal hope) and the immediate union of the heart with its fulfillment (eternal hope).

" . . . a desire fulfilled is a tree of life"
(Proverbs 13: 12b)

It is the dimension of the eternal that promises fulfillment to the heart--the temporal is only an appropriate expression. The triumph of faith rests in the knowledge that it is not within the power of the temporal to limit the fulfillment of the heart--merely its expression. It is a delusion of the first rank to credit the chains of temporality with the power to increase the fulfillment of the heart. This would make love a contingency of fate and the caprice of geography. Better then, as in the days of Augustine when baptism was deferred until just before death in order to have the greatest value, defer marriage until love has exhausted its possibilities in order to gain an unthreatened value.

The heart has its own wisdom and will not confuse fulfillment with expression. The tree of life is not gained by patience (time) but by faith (eternity).

It is sickness of the heart to have both the tree of life and frustration of temporal expression.

In which case the sickness is its health.

JUNE 7, 1962

Much has happened since I wrote the few words concerning the self in relationship. It has not seemed long--but new dimensions of relationship have been experienced.

Before I explore the concept of self as structured by Kierkegaard, this poem by Phyllis McGinley demands space:

"Stay near me. Speak my name.
 Oh, do not wander by a thought's span,
     heart's impulse, from the light
We kindle here.
You are my sole defender
 (As I am yours) in this precipitous night,
Which over earth, till common landmarks alter,
Is falling, without stars, and bitter cold.
We two have but our burning selves for shelter.
Huddle against me. Give me your hand to hold.
So might two climbers lost in mountain weather
On a high slope and taken by the storm,
Desperate in the darkness, cling together
Under one cloak and breathe
     each other warm.
Stay near me. Spirit, perishable as bone,
In no such winter can survive alone . "

The poem is given the title "Mid--Century Love Letter." The context is our contemporary world and especially the bleakness of a cosmos that yields no meaning to the probing fingers of curious man. The movement is not erotic. The self reaches out not so much for expression as for identity. In true poetic style, the self is defined as part of a relationship. Left alone, it has no existence.

Now this is all that I mean to say--and I fear

that I cannot say it half so well. But what moves me is not the desire to enhance the idea with rhetoric but to discover through my own expression this truth.

Of course, I am not searching for existence--I am writing from within it. If I were not 'in relationship' I could not search. Which is to say, if I were not a 'self' I could not define self. There was a time when I prized loneness (not loneliness) as the sanctuary of self--I built my wall. I no longer fear the world. I have my insecurities, but they are only because I fear to be misunderstood. It is much worse to fear being understood, and this was the reason for the wall.

Why should one fear being understood? Is it because understanding is an invasion of the secret heart? A breaking down of the uniqueness that keeps me from being lost in the statistics of humanity?

This cannot be the extent of the fear because uniqueness does not disappear in relationship nor does self revelation make the sacred common. Somewhere in the primordial self a distortion occurred. The tentative movement of self into relationship experienced pain. Instead of acceptance there was exploitation--the other self found the world a threat as well. Instead of mutuality there was struggle for position. I retreated, wounded, to my own world. The distortion was not my wounds--they could heal; I counted understanding to be a threat -- -- -- enter grotesqueness!

But herein is the pathos of distortion--the crippled image of self reflects its own ideal (and its own reality!). There is no possibility of healing within the horizons of one's own distortions, because there is no disease. Rather, the disease becomes its own obsession with intuitive power to guard against the distortion (!) of being a part of another through unhindered self revelation.

Now the wall does not only depend upon its massive stone for strength--it has cleverness as well. And year after year, cleverness is added to fear and the self becomes an expert at defending its secret. When necessary, mutuality can be experienced to gain mutual ends--but there is always withdrawal at the last minute. The self will not be captured by involvement--the pain of being understood is greater than the need for self revelation.

Have I described the process by which my distortion formed? I hardly know for sure. It seems almost too clear--too obvious. Perhaps this is part of the original distortion (did I not say that cleverness was its strength?). Is it presumption for the self to speak within distortion and to say "now I see clearly for the first time!?"

Indeed it is -- except for one thing: when the self speaks of itself 'in relationship' it has a test for truth. The reason for this is clear. The distortion of the self was precisely that it defined its reality by virtue of being 'out of relationship.' Hence, to be 'in relationship' is to be free of that particular distortion and for the first time, free to measure reality in terms of self concept without the bias of distortion.

This much I have learned: a self concept which cannot be reflected through the perspective of another self (not just any self--but a self 'in relationship') without being altered, cannot be held as real.

What I am saying is that a self concept is not in harmony with reality unless it is consistent with the reality of self in relationship. If the self in relationship is loved--it can only maintain a self concept of 'unloved' by denying the reality of the relationship. But here is where the transformation of unreality into reality is most painful. What happens is that we must become 'different' than we have always been in order to conform to the new reality. This in not easy. We have learned to live with the self concept 'unloved.' It is a familiar face and we are no longer frightened by its grotesque features. In fact, when alone behind the wall--safe in the sanctuary of loneness--its contours are reassuring, its familiarity our only friend.

I have not discovered the self (Kierkegaard will have to wait for another day!), but I have discovered the presence of distortion and the therapy of 'relationship'. I have been understood and I have survived! It is no longer a malignant fear that has sapped the better part of my life thus far. My movements are halting and uncertain. The new world offers so much to be discovered, consumed, shared, that I hardly know where to begin. The therapy has not been a miraculous cure (though a miracle),--I need to be 'cured' over and over again. But I no longer fear -- -- -- it is amazing what a difference this makes !

Two questions I leave unanswered:

If the wall was impenetrable--how was relationship possible?

If I had been 'in relationship' from the beginning--could I have written this ? ? ? ?

". . . oh, do not wander by a thought's span from the light we kindle here."

JUNE 8, 1962

Suffering: the ennobling of pain with an idea. I see that this includes the pain of suffering as well . . .
-- this requires a prodigious idea.

The period of courtly love and the cavaliers sounds rather affected to our modern era where even love has become pragmatic, but it was not altogether a romantic ideal:

"I could not love thee, dear, so much
Loved I not honour more."
Lovelace

The knight riding off to perform that which was duty saw no contradiction to his beloved who must relinquish him. One wonders if she knew as much--but of course, otherwise the words would be an offense. In this case they are only a reminder that both understand that integrity is the better part of love. The reminder is appropriate--for love is possessive by nature as well as ethical.

-- is there such a thing as love without suffering?

There would be no integrity without conflict. If everyone had no desire nor opportunity to do other than that which was true to self and God, that which we now call integrity because it arises out of possibility, would only be mechanical--produced by necessity.

-- by the way

how was Eve able to receive Adam's love without feeling that it was produced by necessity and not free choice ?

-- Adam had no other possibilities.

Was there integrity in the relationship?
--suffering?

JUNE 9, 1962

The building is still--pulsating with life.

Chairs facing the front with neat expectancy.
White flowers, flecked with blue,
recklessly squandering pungent perfume
    with silent elegance.

Friendly organ, patiently waiting
 for caressing fingers to arouse
 surging passion into moving harmony,

-- it is saturday night

My study is warm and glows with the softness of

light and love.

It is not hard to let the thoughts move at will through the corridors of previous moments. The building is not aware of the past--nor anticipating the future. These walls do not create a sanctuary--but they are consecrated. Not with a formal prayer but with a feeling heart. Lives have moved into an encounter with God in the presence of this silent building. Perhaps the walls know more of the silent agony--fear --desire--and hope of those hearts than I ever shall. Yet I know that life has been lived here, and where life has been eternity has related itself to time in the pathos of the human situation.

I am OVERWHELMED with the mystery of life. Such POSSIBILITY! ! ! !

Such REALITY !

Yet, how little understood and accepted.

These seats shall be occupied tomorrow again. Who shall come?

What do they seek? What shall I say?

The Word of God, you say. And what is that? Printed characters upon expensive paper? Ancient monograms hallowed in their ambiguity by the reverence of centuries?

Or does God speak again?

Does Jesus move among us with disarming glance and searching heart? Does He care about overdue bills, interminable pressures, painful memories, strained marriages ?

Yes, of course, but then how does He speak? These words are not precise enough to be discovered in the Scripture.

I am to preach, you say; explain the scripture, say the words that are true to both God and the human situation!

It sounded easy once -- -- -- -- -- -- --a hundred years ago I could have accepted the assignment with confidence, tonight I see the pulpit in its unapproachable fascination. If I could not speak I would not be here. My role is consuming, my mission terrible in its attraction. I cannot resist the reality of that crisis when heaven and earth merge in the "event" of preaching. Yet, having known its reality--I tremble in its recurring demand. So much that is said comes too easily, trite clichés that spin the truth like a top but never move the heart. Over simplified solutions that are easily remembered but better forgotten.

So much is premature. Words must be produced to fill the void of thirty minutes with frightening regularity. There is not enough time to suffer to flee--to return--to believe--to--doubt--to pray--to suffer--to think.

But would I ever be ready? No. And this is the truth that makes an impossible situation possible. The point at which I am ready is the point at which it is too easy--too comfortable--too professional. (I cringe and cannot look at the word!)

The possibility of preaching lies in its necessity (not duty)--the necessity is the insatiable search of my own spirit for that reality of communication between my heart and that one heart--and this with God speaking through it all. Not through me, but through it all HE IS THERE. This is what makes the words true, not their pious ring or pompous tone. (I cringe again!)

I have never entered the pulpit but what my heart burned. I have never doubted that some thought was mine through my own struggle for reality. It has not come early, and has not been extensive (often barely enough to justify a paragraph), but it has never been lacking and I have never regretted a message because of this.

This does not make it any easier to face the

crises--

> only more difficult to turn away.

It takes an hour to say this--but I can think it in a moment! Is this strange? Has every thought so much content when disciplined out of the realm of the infinite into finite expression? Then what great potential there is for expression and what reason to labor to bring the spirit to bear upon the orderliness of time.

I am such a child--so impatient to transcend everything with a great idea!

I will learn and will be trained and pruned to produce, this I know--yet I am grateful for that which cannot be learned--

> the gift of a great idea.

JUNE 14, 1962

It was John Milton who wrote, "A writer ought himself to be a true poem if he wishes to write well . . . in laudable things."

I wish I knew what a poet was. There are so many who pass themselves off as poets who only have some ability to manipulate words and to startle the senses with bold paradoxes.

Of course I do know, Kierkegaard taught me:

"A poet is an unhappy being whose heart is torn by secret sufferings, but whose lips are so strangely formed that when the sighs and the cries escape them, they sound like beautiful music. . ."

So then: if one wishes to write well . . . in laudable things--he must be--before he can say.

Strange alchemy--that pain produces harmony.

Why is it that we linger at the side of the poet? Is it only because of the beauty of his words? No, because our secret suffering reaches out to touch his heart.

I fear that far too many traffic in lessor things than suffering. Not because they despise--they simply do not understand.

It was with interest that I read these words which are close to being a poem:

> As lines, so loves oblique may well
> Themselves in every angle greet;
> But ours, so truly parallel,
> Though infinite, can never meet.

> Therefore the love which us doth bind,
>   But fate so enviously debars,
> Is the conjunction of the mind,
> And opposition of the stars."
>   (Andrew Marvell)

There is the paradox of fate and love--but it is not suffering and thus cannot be a poem. It produces despair and not meaning.

The theme is valid--love as the infinite projection of self. The symbol is clear--lines which parallel but never meet. It ought to be a poem, but it isn't. It has no dimension of eternity to it. It is a mistake of the first rank to equate infinite projection of a line with the infinity of self transcendence.

Love is not a line--it is the perception of self in the eyes of another. If the lines merged into one--what then would there be? Not fulfillment, but confusion.

Now it is true that there is an element of frustration to love, but it is a dialectic of meaning not a parallel of despair. The impossibility of the temporal is what the author meant to convey by the symbol of parallel lines--but blind, envious fate is not the enemy of this relationship, rather, the suspension of the eternal in time is volitional and not a cruel trick. The spirit guards its own reality through appropriateness--but not without suffering. But in this case the suffering is tense with meaning. There is an ecstasy of balance that produces integrity as a strain produces firmness in a muscle.

I cannot hate time -- for time produces poets.

The problem has been pursued yet another time--the answer is the same.

I knew it would--yet I had to work it through once more. The repetition seems absurd yet desperately important.

It is not that you do not remember--but that I might not forget.

We must write well . . . in laudable things.

JUNE 21, 1962

I have enjoyed walking to the church the past few mornings--the car is a necessary convenience but a stranger to awareness. There is much to see and observe. Houses that once flashed by with anonymity now have personality. Front lawns are revealing!

There is the same subtle line between security

and conformity in a person's front yard as there is in his life. The "tyranny of suburbia" is the image of conformity. Each lawn blends into one harmonious carpet of green with permissible variations (a discreet shrub here and there which concedes the weakness of personality without threatening rebellion). The sore spot in this happy scene is the character who boasts large patches of red clay sprinkled generously with a dozen varieties of healthy weeds grown into a matted and uncouth jungle. The first day I prized him as an individual amidst the crowd, but lately I have dismissed him as a slob (I discovered empty beer cans in the crab grass !)

This morning I discovered finer distinctions within the veil of submissive conformity. What seemed at first glance to be a secure and comfortable image of verdant security now moves with seething struggle for status and improvement of position without betraying an alien spirit. The fellow with the white picket fence for instance, there is no getting around it, a picket fence is pretty high up on the scale of satisfaction. It fairly oozes with righteousness. And white--this is almost unfair! There is only one thing to do with such tactics--fight fire with fire!

The old wagon wheel buried by the front porch

made me cringe (another slob!) but no, and here my curiosity moved to admiration; this was a very stroke of genius! He would not strive for a whiter picket fence with a sharper point, but for originality. I could picture it now, rustic elegance, the charming remnants of another generation arranged with nostalgic carelessness. (No doubt at this very moment he was out scouring some shadowy barn for old horse collars and broken wagon tongues.)

The individual amidst this desperate scene is not easy to discover, It may take a few more observations. There is one candidate that I am watching closely. His dichondra looks healthy enough--he is no slob, but the crab grass appears not only to be tolerated but accepted. The ragged edges of the lawn shows evidence of a battle for survival against the trampling of undisciplined little feet--obviously, he lets the kids play on the front lawn! At this moment he appears to have the careless indifference required to be an individual with self assurance of his own image. What he will do when the disapproving looks of the neighbors continue to bear down is another thing. He may well give in and relegate the kids to the back yard. There is no stopping from that point until the white picket fence.

There are casualties also--some crack under the strain.

This morning bore sad witness to another

tragedy. It was enough to make a man cry. I picked my way through the debris littering the sidewalk and tried to reconstruct this crime of passion. It may have begun with a few tentative, halfhearted attempts to free some stubborn crab grass from its love of life. Momentary inspiration may even have created a vision of greater feats (the white picket fence was clearly visible two doors away).

What happened next is forever cloaked in the madness of desperation. Somehow, he got his hands on a roto--tiller. Don't ask me how--desperate men have means unknown to more tranquil minds. He must have plowed through the tangle of the grass and shrubs a dozen times with vicious and destructive hate. It seemed insufficient for him to root up roots--he exposed rocks with defiance of all decency. With insolent disdain he turned his heaving machine around on the edges of his neighbor's lawns leaving a trail of dirt, tangles grass and broken wood (I think he ground up a few lengths of wood with cruel vengeance on the picket fences).

I shall be interested in discovering his next move. If I have him figured right, it will be in the dead of night, and with sheepish and covert chagrin. The sidewalk will be swept hastily and the trash boxed for the refuse trucks neatly stacked by the curb. He might even throw in a little grass seed and add public repentance to his chagrin by trying to raise a respectable lawn. Somehow, I hope he leaves it bare for a few months. A man ought to be allowed some dignity in failure.

What has this to do with relating Jesus Christ to the world? Nothing and everything--in one sense this perspective is a pathetic and poignant reality. Life is not a very noble thing if one counts nobility in terms of moral achievement and righteous virtue. Most of us build with futile necessity nagged by a constant reminder of failure. Even success is a discomfort and prestige a cruel tyranny. If Jesus Christ is the patron saint of virtue and the paragon of righteous religiousness, then the greater part of the world is too weary and sinful to care very much.

I am obsessed with the idea that the truth of Christ lies closer to these lives than to the self righteous theology of the church. Not that I find reality in negation--the church is the historical line of continuity of the Kingdom of God in the world. Yet, the church has a constant danger--that of becoming . a way--but it leaves the church exposed and defenseless. It is simply HONESTY. This is hard enough with the world looking on--but virtually impossible in the pious fellowship.

Perhaps this is a clue to my violent reaction against identity with my own profession. The attend-

irrelevant to life.

Truth is not the fruit of immediacy (contemporary existentialism in literature has lost sight of this)--it has its own existence. However, the tragedy of truth is its lack of incarnational witness. Jesus brought truth to humans through the incarnation of love and redemption. He was not accepted by the contemporary Mosaic structure, but he did not deny his relationship to it. When forced, he always chose the individual over the system. That the system forced him to this choice reveals the contradiction of the system with truth, not the anarchy of his spirit.

It is not that my spirit is alien to the system--but I cannot conform. This is not an easy course. The price is great, not the least of which is the inner questioning of my own life. I think that I fear distortion as much as I do conformity. The humanist has chosen human reality over against a preposterous divinity. It is not to the credit of organized religion that it forced the choice, nor gloats in its self appointed orthodoxy.

I have learned the simple formulas of orthodoxy. All who do not confess Jesus Christ as Savior are lost--turning to Christ insures eternal salvation and immediate release from fear, frustration, and failure. It can be proclaimed with no discomfort and with a thousand inflections as long as one steps up to the crowd and speaks from a box, retreating into the sanctuary of an ecclesiastical bandbox. But to mingle with the crowd! Rubbing shoulders with the individual--this paralyzes the easy movement of preaching and makes it a laborious and prodigious effort. I am immobilized with the problems of taking the simple formula and relating its meaning to the ambiguity of human individualism with its complex meanings.

I am sorry--I simply fail to be moved with the simple statement that my neighbor is going to hell because he does not share my convictions about the theology of Jesus Christ. It is not that I am sure that he isn't--but that it seems too grotesque for words that I must put him in hell before I can love him in Christ! I do believe in hell--for myself at least. That is, I have no illusions about the reality of personal immortality and the possibility of eternal existence as a self without relationship. Perhaps that is why I cling so desperately to relationship.

But my neighbor! Is it sinful (heretical) to give him the benefit of the doubt while struggling to understand him so that he can understand me? He is not impressed with my theological "proof" of his prodigality nor does he think bad of me for consigning him to hell, he merely pities me.

Pity is the iron curtain that keeps the church at a safe distance from the world. It is impenetrable to every assault and secure against every strategy. There is

ant at the gas station this morning almost made me cry with his breezy "Good morning Reverend--fill 'er up?" I could hardly eat lunch two hours later ! The last time I had such convulsions was with a group of ministers in a restaurant in Bakersfield when one of them began singing the Doxology in a stentorian bass before we ate breakfast! He was happy in the Lord I guess--but I almost drowned trying to crawl in my coffee cup.

    To say that I am concerned over my reactions is an understatement. Why I should be ashamed to be publicly identified as a minister has long perplexed me. Others don't seem concerned and this by no means indicates that they are professional or pompous. They simply seem oblivious to that which makes me cringe. It is my perpetual awareness that creates this sensitivity, this I am sure. The reactions of others to the image of ministerial professionalism seems utterly incongruous to the reactions I desire in order to understand them so that they can understand me.

    I simply choose to identify myself with them rather than with my profession. Jesus chose the individual -- I like to think he would have been embarrassed to wear the distinctive robes of a rabbi.
    -- but who would understand me if I dared to share these thoughts?
    but I have . .. .
                 ... . and I am.

JUNE 26, 1962

The air is cool and filled with thoughts--the warm day has yielded to the caresses of the evening with grateful sighs--almost inaudible murmurings, as if even the sounds were listening to the soothing soliloquy of their own symphony.

I remember last evening. It was a moment on the horizon of an illimitable world. The stars sprinkled the heavens with speeding light--racing to its own death, but bravely winking at passers by. The presence of the night was more real than plunging into a pool of water. There have been other nights, but less awareness. How much there is to see--hear--feel--discover of life ! But we are limited by our narrow perspective and need the prompting of mutual awareness to sense the thrill of discovery. The sounds of the night can be filtered out of their inaudible back ground by the patient searching of hearts for something to share. The ear quickly joins the game--the distant bark of a dog, the screech of brakes on a busy street on the other side of the world, the impromptu delight of a child carried in crazy laughter over the drifting currents of the night air, the chirp of a cricket--once lost in its anonymity now is identified, discovered, possessed.

What is life? A concatenation of unrelated sounds welded together by the insensitive ears of impatient people into empty days and silent nights? Is it possible that we miss life in the living? Catapulted from one activity to another by the nagging voice of a desperate doubt--impatient to finish this treadmill so that others can begin--frozen with fear lest we enjoy that which is temporal and hate that which is eternal.

Fear--doubt--and impatience are no friends of the spirit. They make life into an ogre of duty--a distorted, grotesque wilderness where every pathway is a mockery of hope and every spring a pool of sweat. It is bad enough for the world to careen its way through a desperate existence--but when the Christian fights the same ghosts, the heart looks for reality and leaves heaven to the weary and impatient.

For over thirty years I have been pursuing a desperate course with an impossible speed. It is not that I have been misguided--only that I have forgotten to see, feel, touch, and taste. I would not retrace a single step--yet I know that I have scorned a thousand nights in my blind haste. It has always impressed me that Jesus was not pursued nor pursuing. Nothing could interrupt him, nor could anything detain him. He saw every cripple yet passed them up for the cross. He felt every pain of the hungry, the dispossessed, and the sinful, yet had time for his own suffering. There was a time when I would have been satisfied with nothing less than saving the world--now I am more concerned with saving myself. Somehow I think the two are more related than it first appears.

This much I say with grateful heart--my life has merged with my ministry. I no longer fear that my life will take more time than this moment. Sunday night I said this:

If you need more time to find greater happiness--you have placed far too much value on things that are unimportant.

The more I think about it, the less I care about anything else I said. This will stand.

I hear a train--a passing car--some boys walking by . . .

and an answer.

JUNE 29, 1962

"A man's spirit will endure sickness..."
Proverbs 18:14

The human spirit has a capacity for suffering that is not unlike the heart of God. This sickness is not a disease of the spirit but the agony of the heart which can see more than it can reach. And it is just the nature of the heart that it nonetheless does not prefer blindness to sight.

My own heart sways like the wild movements of a suspension bridge in a hurricane--it seems that every connection is ripped from its socket and all stability sacrificed to the wind. At one moment life is an orderly process of meaning within the comfortable security of known limits. Then self confidence trembles with new feelings, new desires, and strange delights. I stagger like a senseless man down a strange street--I reach for the familiar holds and look for well known signs to prove that right and wrong are not distorted and still everything moves. I slide down inclines that have no direction nor end. I look up and recognize nothing. I listen and hear only the pounding of, my own heart and suddenly I discover both depth and height to my life.

My wild careening was not in chaos, but in relationship. The fearful movements were within the resiliency of my own spirit as it sought to find meaning in new dimensions. God is greater than my fear and relationship with Him gives tensile strength to the spirit.

There are two circles of life--not only one. From above (or from below) it appears single, for the two are superimposed in a vertical plane. The upper circle is the dimension of the eternal, the lower is the temporal. The self moves with familiarity in the realm of both there is expressive meaning with appropriate language in either realm. Because of this, the self is one, but not single. With deep perception and honest searching of self in relationship, the self becomes intuitively aware of what it is--a dialectic of possibility within a unity of reality.

The thin line between the two circles is first thought and then felt. Through awareness and experience the circles move apart without separating . . . (though from above or below they appear to be one). The movement is a dialectic. The temporal dimension of self demands immediate fulfillment and advances in the name of self expression. The eternal dimension of self preserves an infinite perspective to every movement of the temporal and suspends expression in the name of self preservation (integrity). The hiatus between the circles constitutes the sickness of the spirit (suffering). This sickness is not an intruder into the happiness of the self, but is self imposed to preserve reality and meaning . This does not deprive the self of freedom--with exquisite abandon, the self moves as one when the movements of the temporal are appropriate to the needs of the eternal.

The self does not consider the suspension of movement a tedious wait--this suspension is itself a meaningful movement which demands all of the passion and seriousness of the human spirit.

And the relationship is preserved.

JUNE 30, 1962

"... but a broken spirit who can bear?"
Proverbs 18:14

This, of course, simply is the self without relationship. What first appeared to me as chaos became growth when the relationship was preserved.

When the suffering of the self in dialectic is

unperceived and unidentified, the reaction is one of withdrawal instead of inward suffering. The self retreats to heal itself alone and sickness is changed into despair as the relationship disintegrates. At first, despair seems to be the more obvious choice--it has boundaries. Even healing through despair appears to be a gain because life becomes possible again--though not a possibility.

I find that suffering is redemptive and renewing. When the movement is one of inwardness in order to preserve relationship (though it is done with an agony of honesty) the sickness is removed from a physical distress to a spiritual suffering--and hope revives, joy permeates, possibility comes alive! But O how hard to bring the failure within the relationship! How much easier to leave it as a failure and to live with the scar.

But a broken spirit who can bear? There is no redemption without relationship. Can there be a relationship with God without one with man? I doubt it. Human relationships are made possible by grace and love. It is not the grace and love that make Divine relationship different--but God. If we deny one relationship--the spirit is broken: grace and love can not redeem.

Relationship is not only redemptive, it is edifying. We move with imperfection and immaturity in trying to fulfill the possibilities of self in existence. Apart from relationship the immaturities become repetitions and the self is frozen in its growth. The love of a relationship that renews possibilities promotes mutual edification (at the human level)--the growth that occurs through suffering makes the relationship stronger and the individuals concerned freer selves. This is a mystery and a problem to the temporal dimension, but a joy to the entire self, which seeks the perfection and freedom of the other in order that the relationship may have infinite possibilities.

I praise God today for the gift of life

-- for the patience He has with me.

I thank Him for loving me in such a way that I can make all the movements of my life before Him-- even imperfect ones.

I abandon myself to the reality of my relationship with Him and will proclaim the thoughts He has put upon my heart with confidence and joy.

DECEMBER 1, 1962

"... a threefold cord is not quickly broken." Eccl. 4:12

Koheleth builds better than he knows (even the most inscrutable providence permits us this occasional moment). The numerical value of a trinity is not its strength. Two are better than one he has already said this. Yet, the addition of a third does not merely triple strength--two have all the strength needed (to be alone when we stumble is the qualitative cipher of despair, and the presence of another is the qualitative numeral of completeness).

The threefold cord preserves the strength of the two without destroying the uniqueness of each. Two can fill the quota of individual need, but unless there is a third there is nothing to prevent the two from destroying each other through fear.

Ultimately, we must have a common faith to dispel a common fear. Trust in another can never be as great as mutual trust in the presence of the third. The dimension of the third bathes the two with integrity and respect--this can never be produced by the will of two. Two can keep each other from falling, but only the third can keep them from fear .

Only three can become one--yet, even here love must slay fear that would limit truth to one (or the other).

And if the upraised sword seems alien to the profile of our god then we are left with only two alternatives:
--re-label our god (perhaps the sword will slay tenderly) or .... carry our god back to the shelf of our desire and wait for it to beckon Us again with its expected {acceptable) plan.

- -but . . . how can one be warm alone?
(4:1)

JULY 25, 1963

It takes no little effort to record the date on this sheet of paper. With December heading the previous entry and June the one before that, the very recognition that time is relentlessly measuring the suspended agony of awareness is a fact that would be easier to ignore.

It is not as though the interval is empty--much has been said and not a little written, but somehow it was necessary that chronology give way to perspective. It was the day before yesterday (6-30-62) that I wrote: I thank Him for loving me in such a way that I can make all the movements of my life before Him--even imperfect ones.

It was as though I had snatched the treasure of truth prematurely from the vault of knowledge. The concepts were too great to be believed and too true to be forsaken. I plunged extravagantly into the stream of experience with no clothing for the return trip. The effort of survival was strength to an insatiable passion for understanding.

Time hung suspended while the facets of truth were turned slowly in quest of unlighted corners-- nothing must be left behind. I have promised myself this necessity. And not even the accusing faces of undated pages will force me to run ahead of myself.

Yet . . . . . the time has come to once more walk on the edge of unbelief.

The strength of truth becomes a weakness if it is not hazarded against the untried. There are things to be said that I know now to be true even though others will fear their implications. I cannot walk both the way of professional security and personal honesty. I would be sorry if forced to be misunderstood--but I will not hedge with understanding.

I no longer shrink before the question: "If love is

absolute, and neither Divine nor human, why are you the only one who speaks in this language?"

The answer is obvious (if momentarily disguised)--there are multitudes crying the same truth. The only problem is, they are without the church and not within. Those whom we have long consigned to the dust of delinquency have outreached us in their need. We shall do well to overtake them with the truth that only now is an echo in the lips of despair.

The Love That God Is will now be written. I care little for its destiny, but only for its birth. It shall be responsible for its own survival. There is no doubt of its genuineness--it has already been understood; I should say that understanding has necessitated its utterance.

My responsibility is not to create novelty, but to unclothe the true. This has always been the more prodigious feat. Kierkegaard was the only one lonely enough to be honest, and patient enough to learn the vocabulary of pure expression.

Now the days shall be counted and the hours bear their interminable toil--for honesty and patience have a great price.

I have been loved--and now have a reason to pay the price.

JULY 25, 1963

Pure knowledge and love are the same experience.

This can be easily demonstrated by pointing to the estrangement that misunderstanding brings. The knowledge of the other that flows from acceptance and grows through uninhibited expression of self to self does not lead to love--it is love.

For this reason, the Hebrew word denoting sexual intercourse is the word for knowing. Yet, intercourse with estrangement is utter loneliness. Those who pursue love through physical knowledge force the self into the extremity of indignity--those who have knowledge of each other but without the temporal possibility of intercourse bear the sadness of unsymbolized expression (expression is not the relationship but the self in relationship).

The limit of our love for God is drawn at the horizon of our knowledge of Him. There is no way to force the spirit past this barrier by vows of spiritual compulsion.

But no one has ever seen God, and this frustration of natural desire easily leads to the illusion that he cannot be known (or loved).

God is love, and those that love, God abides in them. Knowledge is love--the knowledge of another self is Divine, and all the attributes of redemptive love inherent in one relationship: humility, repentance, faith, edification, and the good.

JULY 26, 1963

"You will seek me and find me; when you seek me with all your heart."
Jeremiah 29:1 3

It is strange that we are so easily led astray by a promise such as this. The search for God is a universal quest, though few will acknowledge the object of their pursuit, and even fewer claim much success.

The pathos of life is not so much that so few are successful in their seeking of God, but that so many take this as their first responsibility. Our problem is not finding God but finding all of our heart. The prodigal son never really did find his father, nor did he need to. In the narrative we are told that "he came to himself." Whatever the implications of this may be, at the least there was the beginning of honest self awareness leading to a measure of self-responsibility. At this point his father who had been waiting (love is not sovereign) now was free to claim the son without destroying his dignity as person.

Can God be far from one who has found all of his heart?

I talked this week with a young mother apparently suffering from the tormenting pains of terminal cancer. Her first response was not "I am suffering," but "I am afraid." She has not been told that her condition is fatal (it may not be), but the important thing was that her extremity produced reality--fear is an honest reality, pain is only a circumstance. She spoke of her Catholic background and of answers to prayers through some special saint (St. Anthony, I believe).

It was a refreshing experience to claim with her the promises of God with no need to disprove her faulty theology or heretical aspersions on the doctrine of grace. I have never cared less for the formal declarations of theological truth (though I do not hesitate to define the theology of redemptive love). The reality of her heart was a compelling evidence of spiritual assurance.

I only say this to make the issue clear: there is no God for the halfhearted.

The thought just occurred to me--if all were halfhearted would there be a God? Do we have the power to destroy God by disallowing love?

Could it be that in the creation of humans (the incarnation of love), the being of God was hazarded in the precarious existence of love?

Does God watch humanity like we observe a candle burning alone in the dark--and if the flame flickers out, turn away to another experiment? Or is he the flame?

The questions are naive (not blasphemous) for I speak not against God but for my heart. I do not live in fear of belittling God but of failing to measure the heart. I have desires and fears that seem alien to the good, but the conditions for knowing God are not virtue but honesty. These desires are who I am--yet I am more than desire, I am desire before God. Knowing myself, there is then the possibility of choosing the good (he has left me this dignity). Is the good God? No--I choose the good of self-fulfillment, God must choose himself, I cannot be God--that would be inhuman.

I have only begun to find all of my heart,

there is nonetheless an intimation of God.

JULY 27, 1963

". . . and they heard the sound of the Lord God walking in the garden in the cool of the day . . . ".
Genesis 3:8

The fragrance of evening drifting through my window does not seem especially Divine--but it is easier to listen for the sound of Divinity in the evening.

Perhaps it is the heat of the day causing us to defend ourselves against irritation that makes us so unsusceptible to inspiration at times.

There is something about the quiet evening air in my study that makes me ache with loneliness. Is this why God sought Adam in the garden? Did He know that Adam and Eve would be hiding from His approach?

Why do people hide from me behind the facade of casual friendship? I am not aloof--only numbed by acquaintanceship without communion. It is not possible (appropriate?) to lend the intimacy of self-revelation to the careful vocabulary of fear. The strain of such calculated friendship that leaves the self untouched is unbearable--I retreat to the sanctuary of reflection and send desperate words into the night.

It is the despair of my heart that I have perfected my disguise so as to turn away even the curious. My only defense has been in not needing

    --or caring

    --or sharing.

Oh God--how can I convince them of this untruth!

There is a quietness that comes when the heart has been allowed to symbolize its need--

this could only be through response.

Who walked this evening in the garden of my soul?
    God? . . .
             or a friend?

    --either is sufficient.

JULY 29, 1963

I have been to the end of my life and back.

It was not a long journey--nor a difficult one.

The span of life can be measured by a moment of awareness as well as the calendar of time.

The trip was not taken out of anxiety for the future but the possibility in the present. For only that is possible which can fill the measure of time. We have as much responsibility to be all that is possible as much as to be only what is possible.

AUGUST 1, 1963

A woman's nature is devotion (let it be understood that Kierkegaard has said this).

She finds herself in the complete expression of herself through devotion. But a woman is first of all a person, and it is not true to say that the nature of person is devotion. Pure devotion is the loss of person through the complete act of expression. Thus--devotion is insufficient, and the greater the devotion, the greater the insufficiency. But in this case the insufficiency is not a weakness (for the nature of woman is devotion), but an incompleteness .

The nature of man is faith (Kierkegaard hinted at this but did not explain his thinking).

He finds himself in the security of choosing

himself (believing in himself) in the face of a disintegrating cosmos. His affirmation of self is also an expression, but not as devotion (where the self becomes expression). The act of faith increases self-identity through awareness of responsibility and being.

But a man is first of all a person, and it is not true to say that the nature of person is faith. Faith is the pure incarnation of being through decision, but pure being and loneliness are the same. Thus faith is insufficient, and the greater the faith the greater the insufficiency. Yet, this insufficiency is not weakness (for the nature of man is faith), but an incompleteness.

God created humans in his own image--male and female. This separation of being into two natures was a temporal necessity. Not merely that love could reproduce itself, but that being could re-experience itself through commitment (the two shall become one).

It is not mere mutuality that makes relationship an experience of individual fulfillment--mutual devotion is too extravagant an expression and mutual faith too barren a possession. The incompleteness of devotion is the strength of faith that gives security and protection to the self in its moment of abandonment. The incompleteness of faith is the expression of devotion that gives belonging and comfort to the self in its isolation of being. Now the woman has faith as well as devotion, and the man devotion as well as faith--but one cannot have both complete devotion and complete faith in the same nature.

Through relationship the devotion (woman) is perfectly completed in faith (man) so that there is both expression and integrity in the one moment. In this way the dignity of self is preserved for each as each one completely expresses the self through their respective nature.

The commitment of the marriage vow is the temporal expression of this truth through the physical relationship of intercourse. The possibility of physical relationship is linked with the commitment of a marriage vow (faith understands this necessity). The possibility of personal relationship is linked with self-revelation (devotion understands this necessity). But the person is always either man or woman, and thus seeks to express either faith or devotion in every relationship. Where temporal commitment is impossible, faith still must protect the security of devotion--but will devotion understand this ? Yes--because faith is always security for devotion, and in security, devotion is the fulfillment of self.

Herein lies the sufficiency of the impossible

. . . but only through suffering.

AUGUST 2, 1963

"For if they fall, one will lift up his fellow . . . but, woe to him who is alone when he falls" Ecc. 4:10

It is a terrible thing to fall in the singular.

Yet how often we say of ourselves, "I fell . . ." (or "I failed"). Even when walking with someone we would not be so ungrammatical as to say "We are falling" when only one of us slips.

Koheleth is a clever observer of life. The closest friend will allow us to fall alone so that he might have the virtue of helping us up. But who is so much a part of us who has already fallen when we have slipped?

It is true, as Koheleth reminds us, that the advantage in walking together is that one remains ready to lift the other, yet he did say, "If <u>they</u> fall," and we will not permit him to retract such an intimation of love.

For it is love that makes the construction possible. If one remained standing to demonstrate superior balance, the extended hand would offer indignity rather than edification. There is nothing so cruel as help. It is love that lifts the fallen, not strength (nor truth). And this is so because it is love that falls with the falling (truth could not risk this posture). It is true to love to say, "If they fall," because it is impossible for one to fall alone if he is loved. In which case it is no more a virtue to remain standing because love has already moved with the failure. If the one goes on he has virtue   (he did not fall) but not love. At this point there is no choice, he cannot say, "I am standing," but " we have fallen. "

Of what advantage then is an upright posture? Very much, for the one sees the love that the other momentarily disbelieves (for how can love fail?) Here then is the solution to the dilemma: both fall in the bond of love, yet one has faith (lifts up the other). Faith is not virtue, but the actualizing of love.

It remained for the apostle to state it more simply, "Love never fails."

But who could believe such an improbable truth-- except in falling.

It is a terrible thing to fall in the singular.

AUGUST 10, 1963

" . ., put thou my tears in thy bottle! Are they not in thy book?"   Psalm 56:8

Who would think of saving tears! They are such unlovely mementos of moments we hasten to forget. Ah, but the value of tears is not to the one who weeps, but to the one who cares.

What would be only a vial of self-pity if kept on the shelf with our other secret treasures, becomes a precious token of shared loneliness--a pledge that the weeping was not desolate nor the pain a barren thorn.

It is not pain that we fear--but barrenness.

The life of the spirit pours out of the open wound that is our heart.

The uncontrollable expression of love too long measured out carefully--according to necessity

>is a sighing of the body
>a spending to be spent.

The pain of this extravagance is not the giving but the undesignated gift.

Who is able to receive such an offering?

Only the one who weeps without tears. Whose bottles are empty--whose life is barren and thirsty.

What green thing grew these tears?

AUGUST 14, 1963

There is a form of virtue that is insufferable--and a semblance of modesty that is inappropriate.

Both virtue and modesty are attributes of faith, but neither can be claimed by the self in its own behalf. The clothing of the self may be a virtue if the person is unprotected by love--but what is so offensive as clothing for the sake of virtue in the presence of love?

The one who introduces some quick reminder of a pious truth into a conversation of exploration, not only becomes insufferable in his cloak of virtue, but forces immodesty upon us by stripping the relationship of love. This is betrayal--for we are either forced to clothe ourselves quickly (repeat his pious intonations) or allow the tendrils of our inner self the indignity of exposure to an impersonal truth. It is at this point that truth crucifies love.

There is only one recourse--to cloth ourselves with darkness.

"Let only darkness cover me, and the light about me be night." Psalm 139:11

There is security in this darkness, but no growth. For the self dares not move into relationship lest our immodesty become another's virtue (betrayal). The one thing that is feared is light (love), because the self must become unclothed in order to be loved. But darkness cloaks the fear with its comforting presence and repels the light with infallible modesty.

We are safe from betrayal--but never was safety purchased so bitterly--nor modesty so lonely. The finality of our isolation is absolute, for love must become darkness to be trusted.

"Even the darkness is not dark to thee, the night is bright as the day; for darkness is as light with thee." 139:12

The first moment of our uncovering is a painful thing; betrayal is a vivid scar. Yet we cannot withdraw, for darkness is the last refuge. Nor can we deny the presence of another, whose searching glance is as comforting as darkness, whose uncovering as gentle and modest as our own instinct. It is unbelievable! Darkness is as light! The one who moves close to us does not prove knowledge by exposure, nor love by exploitation. Our refuge is in darkness--yet love has become darkness so that both can become light!

Only the betrayed know the exhilaration of trust--the extravagance of abandonment--the luxury of self expression.

> "Forget not that modesty is for a shield against
> the eye of the unclean.
> And when the unclean shall be no more,
> What were modesty but a fetter and a
> fouling of the mind"
> (K. Gibran, *The Prophet*)

Love is modesty--and to be loved the only virtue.

AUGUST 27, 1963

Life is not kind to the individual--on the contrary, normalcy and conformity are equivalent terms in the vocabulary of the well adjusted.

It is in this sense that I speak of the "curse of

awareness." Nothing can be experienced without being interpreted. Not only does this pose a threat to the "group experience" (aren't you feeling well tonight?), but the isolation of misunderstanding only increases the intensity of awareness .

It is not surprising then, when another is able to share this isolation (how can isolation be shared?) that communication assumes a headlong rush of uninhibited expression. The _need_ to communicate does not follow from the unknown experiences shared (as a child _telling_ things that happened in school), but from the agony of awareness that must be healed through the touching of another's knowledge. It is not that another knows us with such complete knowledge, but that he knows _himself_--this is the knowledge of life shorn of all pretense and unreality. It is this reality that comforts our longing to know someone else, but how can we know one who does not know himself? And if he knows himself, does he not know us too? ? ?

This experience is not possible for the "group experience"--only the _things_ held in common can be discussed, and only so that each is reassured that they are _really_ shared. Opinions are traded like so many recipes, but interpretations of life are left buried in the suppressed awareness of individuality. Only the intimate probing of one who reveals himself threatens this secure adjustment to "life." This threat is easily enough handled by simply relegating the individual concerned to the category of "introvert," and plying him with solicitous questions (what's the matter with you?).

Did I say that life was not kind to the individual? His life is, and is there any other? His suffering is sweet and will not be replaced by the euphoria of "adjustment to life."

And then there are moments of understanding when expression rushes to spend all that has been discovered in one moment.

Who else could afford such extravagance! ! !

FEBRUARY 20, 1964

A point of reference for reality

Inevitably every reason gives way to unreasonable circumstances . The first principle is doubt. Doubt of self that routs dignity with scorn and achievement with bitterness. There is nothing that can stand before this scathing storm--ridicule leads to grotesque shadows upon the wall, cast by plans that were once carefully set in the soil of new beginnings. Even that soil is suspect, for it was ground from the rock of failure by the sharp edges of regret.

Our voice echoes in the cavernous darkness--a chamber of horrors that turns the words of friends into weird laughter that mocks their well meaning solicitations. Can they be so naive as to miss the obvious discrepancy?

Ultimately every belief gives way to unbelievable pain. The second principle is realism. Now we recognize the matter for what it is--folly. To have not only believed but to have had faith in the believing ! Twice fooled--but now this pain bears us on the crest of truth--realism churns the sand into foam, our eyes sting even as our heart surrenders all claim to truth and every taste is grit between our teeth.

Finally every hope gives way to hopelessness. The third principle is death. Even our realism was endurable for the hope of some new thing churned up out of the depth. But now that changelessness is infallibly locked into the order of days, there is no longer reason to deny the thought that has often tempted us into oblivion--death. An imperceptible joining of the crowd--lest they be frightened by the sudden deadness and reject our corpse. (Even death has to avoid the appearance of change--life)

    The logic is unassailable. Doubt brought realism and realism justified death. Not even love can conquer such wisdom . . .
    unless . . . love dares to include doubt as the first principle of faith. And then moves through its own logic, but now forced to move doubt into relationship finds that it is more important to doubt the one whom we have loved as the greater doubt. For how shall we be secure in doubt if someone yet accepts our love?

    We have not doubted until we have doubted the greater as well as the lesser. But love does not fear doubt, for it springs not from reason but from reality. The unreasonable circumstances provide only the first stage of doubt, let doubt go beyond--says love--and doubt love if it dare! But beware--that in daring to doubt there is courage to see the undoubtable. That having scoured absolutely the face of love there is strength to accept the reality of ineffaceable absoluteness. That having granted the realism that doubting gives now unable to reconcile the reality of life .

    Nor can we retreat, chagrined and humbled back into the security of our "dutiful acceptance." For the struggle was not for victory or defeat but for truth. And where truth is touched pain is healed into awareness and hurt turned into tenderness. There is no "lesson" to be learned, no vows to make, no promises to offer, and most important, no past to renounce. That which is past for death, through pain has become part of life for faith. There is no time--no past or future, not even present that shall become past--but only now.

Even so, that which was said a hundred years ago is said for the first time now--
". . . if they fall, one will lift up his fellow;
but woe to him who is alone when he falls."

MARCH 1964

The air tugged gently at my cheeks--the grass reluctantly yielded to each escaping foot.

I could not understand--what purpose was there in such delay?
There was work to be done.

The grass is after all, only a carpet and the air a necessity. It was here yesterday and shall be at my service tomorrow.

Yet, there was a speaking.

The sounds of silence became an audible murmuring.

"Tarry," said the fragrance of the morning, "Do not escape so quickly behind closed doors warm with the breath of life, "Breathe me in--for I was not here yesterday, nor shall tomorrow be the same. All winter's waiting has produced such life--do not go without recognition!"

There was a difference--strange that familiarity should change so imperceptibly into fragrance. The living presence that wrapped its tendrils around my body was a pulsating moment of suspended time. "Yield," said the breeze, caressing my cheek with wanton willingness, "Absorb the passion of the morning before the heat of the day changes desire into duty and awareness into endurance."

It was not easy. The practiced indifference of a thousand trips had worn smooth the path of conscious experience.

The senses were awkward and tentative.
Yet, yielding is intuitive--the learning is the doing.
Intoxication brought clarity to dulled awareness--feeling to numbed extremities of the heart.

An eternity passed while time waited. Nothing escaped--all was known in the reality of its being.

"Let no one return to look for me again--let time have the husk of memory--our rendezvous remains."

Behind the door another voice --

"Good morning! ! !

Had you forgotten?

--the first day of SPRING! !

MAY 12, 1964

"although he was a Son, he learned obedience through what he suffered."
Hebrews 5:8

Only God can suffer--and those whom He loves.

And if it should seem inhuman to suffer, we are not being as humans but as animals, who have pain but no affirmation of pain. Love bears pain creatively--thus all suffering is redemptive .

The great peril of life is that we are only the

problem and God the solution. Like a typographical error, we cling to the mistake that gave us birth rather than accept the perfection that does not need us! There is an instinctive knowledge of pain, and an unerring distrust of panacea. However glittering the phrases that offer freedom from self--we prefer the reality of conflict to the unreality of assumed piety. Those who in desperation claim "spiritual" victory over emotional needs may be simply experiencing psychological repression supported by theological concepts. Behold we are sterilized! Spiritually aseptic--capable of neither pain nor desire! If this is faith (and God) then we will oblige--call us unspiritual if you must, but leave us the dignity of at least being lost!

But how much reality can be born without despair? When does death itself become a frightening comfort--or narcotic a necessary anesthetic? Where is there some action--some task--some tangible deed that will sufficiently claim our passion without betraying our hope?

Behold--there is suffering.

God comes to Us in the reality of our frustration and does not force us to deny that which is real to affirm that which is merely true. We know what is true, and need not even a Divine reminder of that. If our needs have become our compulsion, at least He knows and accepts that need (His image in us). Meeting us in our frustration he leads us to suffering rather than solution. If this pain be the altar that demands our life, then he leaves us to choose it rather than fight it. Like His Son, who found the cross unacceptable, though inevitable, so we examine the alternatives and choose the pain.

There is no other course which deals honestly with the facts. Suffering turns our emotions into redemptive grief--our tears into healing waters that cleanse the wound without forgetting the pain. We shall never be the same, the loss will never be repaid, the love never substituted--nor do we really want that. No substitute is worthy to replace the grief for what has died. But left to make the tragic hour a part of our life, suffering weaves the rent sadly into the fabric of faith. From deep within ourselves comes feeling greater than emotion to direct emotion into redemptive grief; a deeper grief than unrequited love to transform love into wisdom, and wisdom into joy.

We may never laugh again without a tear, but we will love again. And not with love that moves with desperate anxiety--with compulsive need, but love enriched with suffering. Love that leaves the other free to love, knowing that only such love is worthy of the name, only such love a sufficient relationship,

And who taught us such wisdom? Only Him who learned obedience through suffering. And is suffering a sufficient action? It is the only action all else is an idle gesture in the face of time.

There is this about suffering, this ground need not be fought over again. The moment and the victory is ours--this altar is unalterable .

AUGUST 6, 1964

THE WINGS OF A DOVE

"O that I had wings like a dove! I would fly away and be at rest; yea, I would wander afar, I would lodge in the wilderness, I would haste to find me a shelter from the raging wind and tempest." Psalm 55:6-8

FAITH

The pinioned flash of white against blue
 steals an involuntary sigh from this pedestrian pilgrim.
Does my soul soar into the freedom of flight
 or is longing giving way to illusion?

This I know--the fabric of life wears thin with constant handling

Choking dust rises from the footsteps of pain;
The chain of circumstance bends weariness into despair.

Gentle dove, like my spirit,
hasten above the muddy earth
to the transparencies of heaven!

Are the aspirations of the heart a weakness of imagination--or the wings of the soul?
There are weaknesses I know--
The one imagines dove's wings to be a temporal advantage and bargains one situation for another--but even wings tire of indefinite movement. The other refuses reality to the inconvenient moment and creates dove's wings of visionary escape--but whither shall I flee from myself?

Gracious dove, with my heart, carry hope beyond the vanity of vision into wisdom.

Could it be! This dove--like my soul--not escaping but returning!

This too I know--

"God has put eternity into man's mind." (Ecc. 3:11)

The struggle of the spirit is the longing of a greater reality--

the finding of spiritual identity.

Doves wings are faith--
> In faith we spread the pain of our life across the bosom of his compassion.
> Through faith we lift the depth of our need to the height of His love
> By faith we traverse the wilderness of doubt in an instant of experience.

> Glorious dove,

O my soul, quench joyfully the thirst
for God aroused fitfully in the heat of the day.

"Come to me all who labor and are heavy-laden, and I will give you rest. Take my yoke upon you, and learn from me; for I am gentle and lowly in heart, and you will find rest for your souls." Jesus of Nazareth (Matt. 11:28-29)

DECEMBER 1, 1964

"By mere words a servant is not disciplined, for though he understands, he will not give heed."
                                        Proverbs 29:19

We deceive ourselves in our understanding--for the moment, the exhilaration of new insight seems actually to have changed our position. Yet, the pattern of our life carries on as though determined by some inward compulsion. The reality is this--we change so imperceptibly, even in the most dramatic crises of understanding, that the ordinary patterns of life do not reveal it.

The agonizing truth compels me to listen--for all the words that I have spoken, for all the understanding that I have patiently brought to birth in those who have listened for several years; for all of those who have understood me in my speaking, I have only this to acknowledge: if any have changed, it is only to change into who I am in the inner man. The peril of understanding mere words is not that it is futile but that in the process of understanding one becomes like another through the imperceptible discipline of relationship. Herein the peril is also the promise change (growth) is a possibility, but who can bear it?

The only profile of my ministry is the dimension of reality and truth in my own life. What is reality and what is the definition of truth? I could assume the righteousness of Christ as a substitute image for my own inner life--and without fear say that when others become like me they are becoming like Christ. This would be easier, that is, if I could accept the initial unreality of self-crucifixion, but in actuality it is distortion. People do not become like who I say that I am--but who I inevitably and existentially am.

Nonetheless, it must be that Christ is involved if there is reality of change into the good. If, instead of the righteousness of Christ as a mental substitute for my own reality as person, I acknowledge the existence of God in the inner movements of my own awareness, and this I claim with assurance in that Christ did send the Holy Spirit, his own spirit into my life, so that the estrangement of myself from myself and from God could be bridged; if then I acknowledge the presence of God in my movements, those who become a part of me through that perilous exchange of selves involved with genuine relationship, cannot escape being involved in the reality of God in a redemptive way.

But what are the conditions of this reality? It is too late to speak of perfection and righteousness--these never belonged to me, either by birth or choice. There can only be left honesty, which is a form of integrity equal to righteousness.

Nor can this honesty come disguised as some quick purging confession of sin that gives the sensation of atonement without the reality of transparent genuineness is essential to honesty .

"Purity of heart is to will one thing."

I am indebted to Kierkegaard for a definition of integrity.

The obvious question has the easiest answer--what is the one thing? Anything! For the oneness is the absoluteness with which it is grasped, not the quality of that chosen. It is the good of course that comes into being when we reach that absoluteness of will that makes us a complete person in the moment of will. This is the discipline--refusing to make a distinction within integrity.

NOVEMBER 4, 1965

I wrote once of "the great idea," perhaps more out of desperation than vision. There had to be a unity within the diversity of truth.

I now see that my first movement was one of choosing reality over truth, and thereby forcing truth to be revealed through the prism of reality.

There was a glimpse today of that "idea"--the slightest opening in the wall through which a fragment of a whole could be seen. Behind the reality of my being, stands the being of God--infinitely extending as a personal being through the center of my own soul. There is the being of God beyond my own--separate, yet extending through love inseparably a part of my reality.

There is the reality of "another" a thou to whom my being responds as I. In the recognition of the uniqueness and reality of the other, whom I know as thou, a relationship exists that is love. Not love primarily as affection, gratification, or even expression, but love as knowledge, and the trusting of that knowledge by the abandonment of my being to the reality of thou. In this relationship the entire dimension of God is revealed. Not concealed, nor constrained, but revealed--infinitely revealed so that He is always "beyond"--that is--standing behind the reality of both I and thou, and yet lying between the reality of personal beings who directly acknowledge the other.

I do not love everyone, nor am I loved by everyone. Yet, I do look for the "thou" in others and so strive to "love my neighbor as myself."

All reality is a finger pointing to God. Each fragment of humanity, even that portion that can only die is a reality that confirms the "great idea." Having once made the commitment to reality as the univocal point in truth, the experiencing of life and the reading of creative expressions of that experience does not disintegrate (fragment) me nor simply tear without mercy, but confirms again the ultimacy of love as the reality of God (myself) .

I do not strive for the uniqueness of being God, but I no longer distinguish between His reality and my own.

NOVEMBER 30, 1967

"The king's heart is a stream of water in the hand of the Lord; he turns it wherever he will."
Proverbs 21:1

AND WHY DO I FEEL LIKE THIS TODAY!

The flow of love in my life bends my heart with irresistible grace to meet a response already prepared for recognition. But it is more than recognition or response.

I have experienced this before, painfully, gratefully, believingly.

TODAY I FEEL GUIDED, DIRECTED, SURROUNDED, BY A FLOWING FREEDOM OF

LOVE PERFECTLY CONFORMING MY HAPPINESS TO A PURPOSE GREATER THAN MY DESIRE.   THERE IS SUCH OVERWHELMING . . . TRUST ?

    Is that what I feel?
              YES ! ! !

    I said once that knowledge and love are the same thing. But it is trust that makes knowledge a guided gift. To trust oneself completely to another, even without that one's complete knowledge, is to trust <u>oneself</u>! To love oneself! And then to abandon oneself to the creative purpose of love that binds oneself to the great idea.

    Perhaps there was a time when the idea was only desperately willed by my own existence, or at least seemed to be, but there is a substance now of those who believe the love that God is. And not only represented by those who stayed to see and those who are coming to discover, but those who are part of the stream that flows through a hundred channels.

    This is the incredible truth: that my own heart is being guided like a stream into the crevices of human lives through unimaginable forces and imperceptible sources. It came to me with a clarity that drenched me with wonder and excitement--my life is an instrument of a greater love and a greater idea ! !

This is what the king knew!

This is what only the king could know, and thus yield to the sovereignty of that knowledge--yes, to trust. And even more--to be able to share that knowledge with another, or even better, to discover it together, trust it together .

Now I know why I feel like this today!

AUGUST 31, 1968

There are some who would say that it was not wise of God to place Adam and Eve alone in the world.

But God decreed that it was good!

He gave them no law save that of wisdom.

"Love," he said, "But in loving be responsible to all the possibilities of love."

"Eat," he said, "But in eating choose, lest you be consumed by unlucky appetites."

"Live," he said, "But in living bring both dust and spirit into every movement. "

Virtue without wisdom is uncertain integrity and a barren quest.

For I ask you--is it wise to know of love but not to love?

There is not sufficient warmth in the whole realm of truth to ease the chill of one lonely moment.

It is the wisdom of the heart that leads us to sin against the truth in order to complete ourselves in love.

But can this be good!

I know this--it cannot be good to have only virtue.

For God did say--I heard him--"It is not good for man to be alone."

The simple equation of life into right and wrong reaches only to virtue, not wisdom.

It is not good to be merely right (righteous) nor is it good to be wrong (guilty). So then, good must lie beyond both right and wrong in the wisdom of faith.

The sin of Adam was not that he lacked virtue nor even that he was wrong, but that he was not wise.

He failed to bring to his moment of crisis the wisdom of both dust <u>and</u> spirit. He surrendered responsibility for himself and let something "happen" for which there was no rescue by the spirit.

Here then is wisdom--not to surrender freedom. To be wise is to be responsible to keep every passion and purpose free from the historian of our lives. That which becomes subject to the law of truth (right and wrong) cannot be redeemed from the merciless grasp of those who condemn (for they are right!).

How love has died when it only becomes a fact!

This then is sin--to say: I am no longer responsible for now I am guilty. I have lost my freedom therefore I have become part of the process, no longer able to choose.

There are many things which are impossible for one who is wise. But--and this is momentous--he is free to choose these impossibilities as good! For it is good to be wise.

Adam and Eve lost their innocence because they were unwise, though virtuous. But having lost innocence, is wisdom enough? Yes--because wisdom is the good of both dust and spirit, it is of God.

It is no longer possible to be innocent. For I am not a child whose simple categories of truth are still intact through ignorance of the reality of love. I can no longer sleep with my brothers and sisters. I have eaten of the tree of the knowledge of good and evil.

And yet I will say that it is better to be a man than a child, even as it is better to be loved than to know of love. It was not the loss of innocence that caused Adam and Eve to hide from each other behind fig leaves and drove them deep into the garden away from God, but the lack of wisdom. Having eaten of the tree, it would have been wise to seek their friend--God, Who himself is the accomplice in the act of love.

Satan spoke more than he knew when he insinuated, "eat--for you will be like God!", who loves promiscuously and is not innocent! Ah, but He is wise, and good! And he continues to trust Adam and Eve alone in the world, who no longer being innocent, yet have this law--

        be wise.

NOVEMBER 11, 1968

From S. Kierkegaard's journal notes:

"May, 1842 . . . And it was the delight of his eyes and his heart's desire. And he stretched forth his hand, and took hold of it, but he could not retain it; it was offered to him, but he could not possess it alas, for it was the delight of his eyes and his heart's desire. And his soul was near to despair; but he chose the greater suffering, of losing it and giving it up, to the lesser, which was to possess it without right; or to speak more truly . . . he chose the lesser suffering of being without it rather than to possess it at the cost of his peace of soul . . . and strange to relate, it came to pass that it was for his good."

If I could have only one truth to guide me through life, it would be the truth of "the greater suffering!" For all that is good issues from suffering for the right thing. And yet this truth can only be pressed to the heart as paradox. When the paradox is resolved there is no longer any possibility of suffering, for greater suffering is only greater unhappiness. But through paradox, greater suffering is suffering for the greater value and this yields joy for it is the uniting of ourselves with eternity through decision.

Now there are those who do not understand this. And they hold that all such talk of suffering is morbid and depressing. I suppose then that they have what they want. But why then do they not have joy? The truth of the matter is that they do <u>not</u> have what they want, or if they do, they realize that they will not always have it. Thus they are left with suffering whether they like it or not! But this suffering cannot be willed with the heart, but must be medicated like a headache. Now I understand why my suffering makes their head throb!

No one will understand or share my joy who has not become part of my suffering. Not as one who observes my struggle to relinquish, but as one who relinquishes in order to choose the greater good. There is no room for sympathy in suffering, only joy.

So let the joy be shared! And if this produces even greater suffering is this not the confirmation that the good has been touched with the heart and continues to intersect our lives with eternal significance?

Lord let my suffering be so perfect that all are drawn to thee through my joy.

FEBRUARY 28, 1970

I have just written a letter of resignation as Pastor of the Covina Evangelical Free Church.

How is that possible?

I love these people! And it was I who taught them to trust love, and led them to trust me. But not really to just trust me--to trust God, who always stands between us and in our love.

It is the wisdom of love to sense the distinction between separation and parting. Parting has a finality about it. A looking back with longing and looking ahead with loneliness. Parting longs to forget while separation continues to know.

Separation does have its sadness. But when the interval between "I" and "Thou" has become elongated through separation, it is the sadness which serves as the strength of love to bind together now--and then. For sadness does not look back but forward.

And this is strange! My sadness is also joy! But how can they know that?

And will they understand my joy or interpret it as betrayal? They will understand, for I know how to love--even in separation. And, most of all, that which has been true from the beginning, though dimly perceived, will now become a vibrant reality. It is the good which stands as the third point in love. And God is good. And we shall know more perfectly the good. And our hearts will be comforted.

And I must say--do not fear separation, for there has always been separation even when we have been pressed most intimately together. In this separation faith has always worked to prevent the illusion that we have a hold on each other.

If we allow separation, nothing can be lost. For separation is but the tug of eternity on our tethered lives.

Lord I am free!

⚜ Soulprints ⚜

PART TWO

Wild Flowers and Wanton Words

"Now that my vulnerable leaves are cast aside,
There's nothing left to shield, nothing to hide.

Blow through me, Life, pared down at last to bone,
So fragile and so fearless have I grown!"
      Ann Morrow Lindbergh

LARA
MAY 9, 1970

Awakening to life
Out of the sleep of eternity,
I knew you!

Your heart and mine once shared
A common flow of life;
The one who stands between us
Has taken from me and given to you.

And so we meet at last!

Separated from the warm dream
of life
to risk the dangerous game of
I and thou
But have no fear--
I know you!

Slumbering in your soul
Are great wide spaces
 Of blue skies
 Golden fields
Green pastures--you were there !
You know the feel of rain on bare skin

    the warmth of sun
        the glow of night
            the feel of soil
                the smell of a storm!

Hidden in your heart
is a timeless loneliness
Excavated by the suffering
Of the Individual
You are to become.

Barely now discernible
In gentle murmurings
And pursed lips
Is the untamed fierceness of a spirit
sufficient to be born
And to give birth
To live
And to say YES !.

And when you know all this
And believe it
And when one who loves you
Calls you by name,
Then you will know
That you are
                LARA

JOSHUA RAY
June 8, 1973

my son
you seem to be trying to tell us something
with your marvelous
moving face
which makes smiling seem like a friendly explosion!
we are unused to the language of Canaan,
but our fathers dreamed dreams
and we have seen visions.
and there is something of that in you
but more specifically
is that the redness of grapes I see
upon your lips?

my son
we have come a ways from our beginnings,
and we have left nothing behind but the years
of timeless toil, and the tears
which finally reaches heaven's shore.
you know that we carry the bones of
our father, to his home
and to our peace.
we have everything with us, and in us
that matters, and we seem to be

moving in your direction; though it appears
we shall be taking the long way home.

my son
you are not incredible to me.
your free spirit is drawn from a deep well
of moving, living men.
your gentleness is born out of a fierceness
of faith, an intensity
which does not frighten me.
and when some Moses, seeing the lengthened shadow
you cast among your people, lays his hand upon you,
and when the aweful weight of the NAME
becomes your joyful burden,
and when the still standing wall between us falls
then you will know that you are

                        JOSHUA.

TONDI
April 6, 1981

Grandparents are uncommonly fine
  at filling old photographs
  with strange and unlikely faces,
Who peer out at us without a sign
That we have guessed their secret--
  it was their loving that put us in our places.
And you, child
What answer do you give--what do you say
  when summoned to account
  and asked to explain such a happy face?
Who taught you the secret of holy play?
Was your soul, fresh and new, brushed by
  some angel's wing that left its trace?

Perhaps your name is a partial clue,
  or had you thought it only a convenience
  in finding your present under the tree?
You took a chance on being human, it is true,
But now you are named, and it is a little late,
  for there is a conspiracy between you and me.

Some part of us (I am told)
  waits to be born in tomorrow's child
I dreamed a dream and cast on you the spell
Of awakening to a life that's both new and old,
And living with the haunting happy thought
  that you know more than you can ever tell.

And so, child
When the familiar eyes in the strange face
  peers out at you from the gallery
  of grandparents you have known,
And when you suddenly sense, without being told,
That part of you is ancient, wise in the
  ways of the spirit;
And when you reach the promised land
And it is yours, to keep and to hold,
And when you realize that it is a gift,
And that it is your own life, and it is good,
  then you will know
      why you have come
      why you are here
      and who you are to be;
Then you will know that it was for this (and for me),
  that you are

          TONDI

BRANDON
January 5, 1990

Alive!

Torn from the perspiring flesh of others
we scream our pain with fresh-born fears
and reach out blindly for our mothers,
who bind us close with love-torn tears;
    a baptism into life.

Chosen!

Twice wanted means twice blest!
a first birth born with love's consent
to give you life and prepare what's best,
a gifted birth and second advent;
    a baptism into family.

Christened!

In script invisible to all but grace
the water traces out your name;

I write God's image upon your face
and touch your soul with Spirit's flame;
   a baptism into Christ

Storied!

From those who story childhood days
and show the way to heavenly things,
your night is filled with morning rays
and angels touch you with their wings;
   a baptism into faith.

Destined!

The promise given, the trek begun,
the child's last long look toward the earth,
remembers love and becomes a son,
to experience at last another birth;
   a baptism into heaven.

BROGAN
January 15, 1991

The wind bends low the golden grain,
and blends the scent of air and earth;
in swirling clouds and smell of rain,
a sensuous womb for an infant's birth.
    I am Summer's Child.

A harvest moon hallows the sky,
bathing wounded earth with mystical art;
in the lonely night the wild geese cry,
singing siren's song in a small boy's heart.
    I am Autumn's Child.

As drifting snow quilts the frozen land,
in a storied stable, a quiet diversion;
on Christmas eve the cows all stand,
birthing Christ again in a young man's vision.
    I am Winter's Child.

Our children sow their precious seed,
in flesh covered soil, watered by tears;
a child is born, by an ancient creed,
and gives his youth to an old man's years.
    I am Springtime's Child.

For you, my son, I've lived the seasons,
in you, my child, my spirit grows;
in your heart are all the reasons,
why God is love and surely knows
    that you are BROGAN!

NATHAN
February 10, 1992

There are rolling hills toward which I glance
where prairie winds move the grass to dance
in celebration of sacred vows,
the rooted rhythm of a chlorophyll chorus line,
quite oblivious to the roving advance
of the grazing cows.

I choose the leeward side of the sloping hill
and lay where the close cropped grass still
smells sweetly of bovine breath;
I staunch the bleeding of the severed grass
with my cheek, and promise never to kill
what lies this side of death.

A spirit from the depths of God's eternity,
stirs the stillness of what is yet to be,
a birth to bless this temporal place;
I feel the touch of an infant's breath
brush 'cross my cheek, and rise to see
myself in his boyish face.

Thrice removed by each generation
our lives are linked by each separation,
we meet in those we love;
For you, my son, I've claimed heaven's promise
and embraced on earth the joyful consummation
of God's gift from above.

The wind visits the same green hills, if by chance
the cows still graze and the grass will dance,
but the boy has left his lonely station;
when you see his face in your own reflection
you will recognize in his knowing glance
that you are NATHAN!

SCOTT ANDREW
October 4, 1994

Few are the days and many the years
  that bind our hearts in common birth.
Precarious and precious, the moment nears
  when we are destined to meet on earth
      face to face.

What will we say? What language shall we use
  to loosen our tongues and set our spirits aflame?
Strangers, yet kin, we can be friends if we choose
  to meet with open face; speaking each other's name
      with kindly grace.

Catch in my eyes a distant glimpse of Dakota skies,
  and see the flash of light as thunder clouds form.
Feel the stir in my soul when the wild geese cries,
  and stay with me through the coming storm,
      that hides my face.

There is too little time for us to tame;
  there are too many stories to tell.
You will see my face and hear my name,

but only in heaven come to know me well
face to face.

When you awaken to find your special place,
and know that God has chosen well;
When you see your soul in another's face,
then you will hear what I tried to tell,
you are SCOTT!

TODD
October 26, 1994

Oh Todd, you are beautiful! My child, my joy.

Perfect was your birth; unblemished,
every finger and toe alive with eager longing.
You arrived wearing your very own face,
a mirror reflecting human love,
and a window into the face of God.
You outgrew boyhood boundaries;
searching the silence of mountains' majesty
and the wordless love of common humanity
for an echo of your own voice. At last,
you heard it through the pain
 and found it where it had ever lain,
at home.

Oh Todd, you are beautiful! My brother, my friend.

Perfect was your life, at last,
with all imperfections healed through the
Christ-like offering of your own body
for our devotion.
You found us in finding yourself, and created
the bond we were born to be.
Stripped of all pretense and sibling pride,

your lucid words were spoken clearly
and heard by us who loved you dearly,
at home.

Oh Todd, you are beautiful! My son, my teacher.

Perfect was your entrance into life eternal
wearing your very own face, so loved on earth,
so dear in heaven that Angels wept with joy
at your arrival.
"Come!" Said your new found friend. "Come with me
to the place I have prepared."
"Yes Jesus," you replied.
Your final words of love, a benediction,
 released to live again with our permission,
at home with God.

Oh Todd, you were beautiful in life and in death.

TO EVE, ON HER BIRTHDAY

You touch the mystery of me behind my face

So unerringly, that all desires are accounted for.

Your fragrant warmth seeps through my frozen door

And passion tumbles unmolested into the space

Which loneliness has left without a trace.

My vast sea of love at last, bounded by your shore

Creates a thousand beaches you've never known before,

All are waiting for our coming, each one is the place.

And now at last comes incarnation.

Fragments fall from exploding fantasy

Between us, heavy laden with consecration.

Spirit breathes, flesh conceives reality

That is not consumed in consummation.

I will call her woman--born in ecstasy.

FOR MARY

who has chosen the good portion,
  which will not be taken away from her
  (Luke 19:42)
the thousand fragments gathered up in one moment
    of response
are not strange to those who know you,
    and love you,
      when allowed to exist, one by one.
the strangeness is the fierce and frightening
    totality
of one's random possibilities when summoned
to embrace in one encounter the incredible
    gift of life.

            helplessly,
you choose the freedom which chooses you,
and love the face that exposes the unknown
    meanings of your own name.

            fearfully,
you trespass the open spaces that suddenly
stretch toward a new intimacy,
    while there hangs in the air
the ominous portent of a destructive desire
    or a deeper truth,
      who can say what is good when the rules
        no longer work?

you, who could never be imprisoned by a domestic
    habit,
have always been escaping,
only to be tamed by a wildness
that will not be named
    among the public virtues.
but you are stronger in captivity,
    and while he speaks
there is the promise of peace.
for that, you bear the envious scorn of all the
    Marthas
who could abide your profligacy
but never your efficiency
    to do their work as well.
not being able to disown you,
    they can only seek to bind you
        to their fears.
out of no lack you craved for more
and out of no need, loved that which could only
    bend your heart
into unimaginable shapes of suffering
        and joy.
and because of you,
    one man loves his loneliness
        with its god-like quality
shaped to the exquisite dimensions of an utterly
unique and imperishable knowledge
        of another.

he too, is naming his good, in naming you.

but even as he is speaking, he knows
the good portion, as well,
- will be crucified: but strangely,
this knowledge renders
the senseless moment of separation
even more intensely hopeful.

for here,
in this kitchen, in this home,
the unimaginable terrors are domesticated
by one who listened
and believed.
and now the meal becomes a sacrament
of our remembered future.

A STONE FOR MY HAND

Between two unnatural things
    Such as flesh and stone,
There comes a strange affinity
    Not at all unlike
    A specific gravity
Designated to be the counter
    Balance of time to eternity.

This hand-held peace
    Will deny the rumors
        of the mind
    That dust and spirit are
        of another kind
    And having lost innocency
    Will forevermore
        remain behind
To mark the intersection
        of then and now.

YET NOT MY WILL
Luke 22:42

The sacrament of love

was once a sacrifice

of need on the altar

of blind obedience to the insistent will

that filled the cup far too full

for one swift draught and still

survive the taste of pain.

The renunciation of the plan

was not taken seriously

by the countenance

of absolute love, strangely impotent until

the struggle weakened into strength

sufficient to choose a death and still

survive the birth of love.

I COULD WEEP

I could weep

For the untouched moment that slipped relentlessly
    into time
While we pondered the inescapable truth

I could weep

In bitter regret for the names of unborn children
Who play In streets we have never claimed

I could weep

Inconsolably, for the unspoken phrases
    prepared eternally
For the new discovery of self within self

But I cannot weep

For tears are temporal things
Unused to such exquisite sadness such as fills the heart
Through communicated loneliness

And I dare not weep

For faith must see the image of its own being
Undistorted, unclothed of past and
 Unclouded with future... reflected purely in the other

Yet I will weep

For the insufficient expression
     to replace a tear.

INCARNATION

              When hands hold
The estranged intimacy of alien worlds
each alike in recognition
saddened by the truth untold;
The heart that binds the two in one
Bears inwardly the agony--
Suspended painfully, in one swift pendulum
            of love.

              When hands mold
The awkward edges of a new beginning,
feels spirit stir within its dust
unsure of hope that seems so bold;
The heart that speaks the truth in love
Shares silently the ecstasy--
Reflected mutually, between the echoes
                of response.

A SENSE OF. CREATEDNESS

                              Created things
Leave spaces   in the life of the creator;

The unabsorbed emptiness remains
As the residue of love--when

    Words enveloping the spirit of a thought
        are heard, received, believed--when

    Experience becomes a shape with proportion
        and color, only to be recognized
        and possessed by its new owner--when

    Children, painfully familiar in the strangeness
        of leaving, casually decide which is
        theirs and which is ours--when

    Man takes the field of earth in stride
        and brings forth fruit, a benediction upon
        his labor wrenched from the alien
        substance of his own nature.

But if in a pause of time, an uncalculated
Moment,

There flutters in the creature
    a sense of createdness;
This prenatal longing and belonging
Will find a receptacle for gratitude
    waiting to embrace this expression
    without demanding more.

    He only wants us to remember our name.

AN ELEGY FOR GOD
II Samuel 23:15-17

from its very conception this gift was doomed
to sprinkle the earth--
    was it water or blood?
too great a need and too much love
conjugate the new verb--a sacrifice presumed
to be a senseless act devouring alike
    the giver and the gift.
a crucifixion of logic
upon the tree of knowledge of good
and evil. therein lies a god entombed
too holy to be allowed to live.
earth drinks in its thanksgiving feast--
    is it water or blood?

the finest gifts are not always consumed
upon the parched altars of ravenous thirst.
renunciation is itself a sacrament exhumed
from eternal immutability: god the dispersed
gathered up again in those who have communed.
out of all our eucharists, this is the first.

A RESURRECTION

a resurrection in 6/4 time
(for John at easter)

words are the grave clothes wound
'round the wound that is now my body,
throttling the throat
against an involuntary cry
that would disturb the living
and raise the dead,
binding arms to breast
 in a frozen attitude of supplication--
my god
another cross!

no easter sermon will ever penetrate
these bloody bandages,
i am doomed, forever
to be entombed
in the very front row!
the arguments for my immortality
whistle through the chinks
of my splintered mind and
wind the wind into a deadly draft--
my god!
i shall catch my death of cold.

well in the end i slipped out wordlessly,

there was this angel
taking liberties with time and spaces
jazzed stone jarred
me free to move
in shelton's sweet time,
his ax was beautifully laid
to the root of my cold wounds,
i must not appear too gloriously alive
for the sake of my friends,
thank god for the scars!

CONSECRATION

"Let it be good"
He breathed, as he kneaded the swirling dust
    into every hope and hue of his own image.
And then, stepping back a bit
From his still-new creation
    separating its fresh consecration
    from his older glory,
He whispered again, to no one
    in particular--
        "It is good!"

But even then as the green world groaned
    and stirred to life
        making minor miracles seem common enough,
The image lost its footing
And set the whole plan ajar--
    the simplicity of good splintered
    into a thousand possibilities
    of greed
        lust
            violence
                vengeance
                    and worst of all,
                        unawareness .

And yet, there was a sliver of hope
Prestressed into the likelihood of ungood,
A scalpel-edge of faith slicing through
    the senseless flesh to the bone
    of consecrated spirit.
The creature, still bearing resemblance
    to the creator,
Embraces every hope and hue with remembrance
In the prayer of consecration--
        "Let it be good."

THE CHILD

    the child awakened
        with the knowledge of love,
grateful also to be a woman
experienced in the ecstasy
    of conception.
the theme of self reoccurring
        in the song of another's heart.

ANNUNCIATION AT ADVENT

I will celebrate nativity

I will turn toward warmth and touch my hand
   to my otherness which comes to meet my night

I will make splotches of light dance across the sand
   and run through the darkness toward the light

I will know incarnation--god with thou enfleshed
   and bear his weight lovingly upon my breast

I will not fear the shudder of the surf, a death
   can be suspended infinitely in the truth of yes

I will lift my face to receive the spirit, a breath
   which breathes my silence into speech--i confess

    my joy

        my love

            my faith

HAIKU

sun-warmed sounds invade
    a rendezvous
    here in shade
the sun spins and dies

        between the cool stones
           and the mid-afternoon
        heat
    a slice of morning air

too bad--this careless
    bee became
    intoxicated
with so much flesh!

        slowly, the crushed leaves
        breathe
        reluctant to release
        the burden of love

    the trill of a bird
    sings obligato
    while passion
    descends into being

falling between two
    spring showers
    a green leaf touched
my lips wordlessly

                  scented with suffering
                      a newly picked
                  peony
                awakened my joy

the smoothly worn stone
    shaped perfectly
    to my palm
heard the mating call

                the night air exhales
                    my meditation
                like incense
            careful ! you breathed me!

green leaves hang human-like
    in dead air
    unknowingly
bound to each other.

TWO SPIRITS

oh god
sweet is the wildness
that tames unconquered spirit
 human flesh inspired instrument
 incandescence
arcs two spirits
across the infinity
of one moment, two names
become one meaning
indistinguishable I and
thou
create each other anew
to live again
the chosen individuality
separate worlds
with no bridge to carry
the commerce of acceptable
transactions
unprotected temples
move anonymously through crowded
streets, peopled with strangers
unaware that the gift has
been given
and received.

THANKS FOR YESTERDAY
John 4:52

        yesterday
joy and pain were equally inconclusive.
faith as well as fever can turn to fantasy
when left alone to contemplate the mystery
of being human. the mind becomes a fugitive
from meaninglessness, and steals away to live
in hope that one Word can bring some ecstasy
of relief. but will the cure be still reality
back home. or is the Word too, inconclusive?

but coming home has drawn up the slack
that inconclusively ties faith to reality.
 it is today--now the fugitive is back
with only a Word to face the practicality
of being human. is gratitude my only lack--
when! when did He touch my humanity?
                yesterday !

MY REASON
Luke 17:15

                    nine reasons
For not turning back, to retrace
The steps of a particular grace
Are sufficient
Arguments
To keep the mind fixed on the cure
To know that one can only be sure
Who finds a new name.
                    nine reasons
For laughing, loving, singing, shouting
For never remembering, never doubting
Are insufficient
Arguments
To keep the heart from seeking the face
Of the one who had the healing grace
To know my name.
                    one reason
To break the unreasonable ranks
Of careless life to pause for thanks
Is sufficient
Argument
To keep the soul fixed on the cure
To know that one can only be sure
Who knows HIS name.

THANKS BE TO GOD

Thanks be to God

When the face of freedom is a land,

With boundaries forged by men unplanned,

who slaked the thirst of freedom's birth

in the providence of sun and soil;

Unashamed to bend the vision to the earth

Kneel, gratefully with faith unshod,

To receive the benediction of their toil,

Thanks be to God!

BOUND TO GIVE THANKS

It is bound to be !

The lavish love of seed for soil

Produced a far too potent ecstasy

For dampened darkness to overthrow

It was bound to grow!

    For locked into the sense of seed

        Lies the extravagance of harvest

I am bound to see !

The seed of faith honestly sown

Bears forth the sower relentlessly

To the harvest heart of overflow

I was bound to know!

    For locked into the grief of grace

        Lies the eventuality of gratitude--

bound to give thanks.

FACES

God left my stained glass
    windows
He disappeared into the
    street
Now I look in every lonely
    face
Hoping we will meet

but all I ever see
are empty faces
looking back at me

God became a man, I'm
    told
Has anyone seen him
    since ?
I cry out in every known
    tongue
Risking my defense

but all I ever hear
are clever faces
laughing back at me

People wearing masks are
    strangers

Hiding God from my
   embrace
Sometimes I tear away their
   disguise
Hoping to touch His face

but all I ever touch
are pretty faces
turning back from me

I was touched by another's
   love
My mask became a useless
   game
And now I know that in my
   face
God's l o v e becomes a name

and all I ever see
are open faces
showing love to me

FRAGMENTS OF THE WHOLE

the projecting rock has rough spots on its surface, just enough to keep a small stone from skidding off if carefully placed

the pattern of small leaves held softly against the blue sky by interweaving twigs
on the point, two men fish, one sitting down motionless, one casting aimlessly
watch out for that broken glass
the nightlight flooded the sides of the mountain with silvery sheen
one candle continues to burn

the patter of sudden rain knocking on the ceiling gives one moment two dimensions, two memories

do bugs really like wine, or did they just "drop in"?
the shiny wet sand is hard and firm between the toes, hand

in hand two sets of footprints measure the boundaries of an experience
the dog is huge! uninvited but not unfriendly
the fourth and fifth seats in the back row are taken, there is a coat on the third seat, yes, my friend, you may sit on the aisle
this piece of wood looks like it has been used before to make a temporary shelter from the sun

the little stream is gone! but peace remains in the shelter of twisted branches that form a canopy where life renews its flow
only wise people drive miles to run together in the rain
out of the morning air is born the sounds of the day
good morning!
it's all right, I am here

SUNDOWN IN SEDONA

She was strolling down the street in Sedona
watching the sun paint the red rock hills
        with lavender fire.
In a few minutes the cobalt blue
would squeeze the light into a sliver of orange
        at the jagged upper rim.
She slowed her pace as though the sidewalk
were a cosmic treadmill with invisible gears,
by which she could delay fantasia's final flourish.
Her companions chattered nimbly on ahead,
        their words coming apart at the seams
        cartwheeling through the empty air.
Verbs going one way, nouns another,
        with too-bright and colorless laughter
        scattering them like magpies.

A window suddenly came alive in a curio
        shop at her elbow.
She stopped and turned toward the light
        as though a fragment of glowing color
        had bounced off the hills and struck her full
        in the face.
There it was.
A bracelet of captured colors lying
        on a green velvet cloth.
It was not something that would have caught her eye

in Nieman Marcus nor caused her to linger
at the costume jewelry counter in the Broadway.
She was, after all, no longer a child
and liked the feel of gold against her skin.
    But here, in this place, at this time,
     it held her gaze with hypnotic power.
She refocused her eyes and stared
  at the image of a ten year old girl
   looking back at her in the window's reflection.
She recognized the street and saw herself
  in front of the dime store in San Marino
  where she passed every day on her way home
  from school.
It was the many-colored glass bracelet in the window
  that she coveted.
Her mother's voice drifted toward her
  from down the street.
   "You don't want that.
    It's just colored glass and not worth twenty
     five cents."
She took it though,
  not actually, but in her mind,
   and put it on the wrist of one of the models
   that she drew in her book at home.
The eyes of the ten year old stared back into hers
  as though to say,
   "don't leave me, take me with you."
She looked again at the bracelet of colored beads
  and saw that it had a watch on it.

She began to tremble
> and her knees felt like water.

"What are you looking at?
> You don't want that, you would never wear it,
> > it's just colored beads.
> Come on, we have to catch up with the others;
> > we're already late for dinner."

Taking her hand he pulled her along
faster than she wanted to walk.
The sidewalk moved under them
> and pulled the darkened sky
> over the edges of the hills
> snuffing out the light like a candle in the wind.

As she looked back, the window went dark.
> But in her hand the bracelet was cool
> > and comforting.
> The watch was running and set to the right time.

Promises come to pass in time
when love is a reflection of the child within.

She decided that she would only wear it
> when she could take the child with her.

A PRAYER

Reach out to me, Creator God,
>   for what is to me an unbridgeable chasm
>   is but the span of your hand extended in mercy.

Shade your glory so that it may cast moonbeams
>   across my night,
>   for I am blinded by darkness.

Come beside me Lord Jesus,
>   and bathe my face and anoint it with oil
>   so that my countenance may shine
>   with an inner peace
>   and radiance that comes from peace.

Flood my soul, Holy Spirit,
>   with an unquenchable fountain
>   of healing love.

Remember my forgetfulness,
>   and rekindle in me the joy
>   of being a child of God.

Heal my memory
>   of all self incrimination for past failures.

Give me permission to be angry
>   when I have been betrayed
>   and to grieve when I have suffered loss.

Listen to me when I pour out my complaints
>   and don't stop me until I am finished,
>   and then ask, 'Is there more?'

Let me get to the bottom of all sadness
>	and the end of all bitterness.
Make me relinquish all regrets,
>	free all the emotional prisoners I have taken,
>	and awaken me as from a deep sleep
>	with the fever gone
>	and a ravenous hunger for life restored.

Through the open door of the resurrection, Lord Jesus,
>	I see the cross and the grave,
>	and they are empty!
I love you Lord,
>	and I lift my voice to worship you.
Oh my soul rejoice.
Take joy my King, in what you hear.
 Let me be a sweet, sweet sound in your ear. Amen.

Soulprints

PART THREE

Pools of Reflection and Wonder

"The angels keep their ancient places;
Turn but a stone, and start a wing!
'Tis ye, 'tis your estranged faces,
That miss the many-splendoured thing."
Francis Thompson

As a boy growing up on a farm in the midwest, I spent many hours alone, often in the fields, with the animals, but also choosing my own special places to spend some hours. In those experiences, I recall a feeling of wonderment and a sense of timelessness.

The membrane that separated my inner self from the larger world that pressed in upon me grew porous. The familiar sights and sounds that filled my everyday world had cracks in them through which the vast and mysterious unknown breathed upon me, filling my soul with a knowledge for which there were no names and a language for which there were no words. I still can hear, if I listen, the cry of wild geese winging their way across the night which awakened this small boy and left him staring into the dark, not wanting them to fly out of my hearing. But after they disappeared, I lay there wondering what to do with the infinite silence which they left in their wake.

The boy thrust his hand deep into the freshly plowed soil. "This soil is your life," his father suddenly said. "You take care of it and it will take care of you."

Years later, having left the soil, and his father, he discovered the wisdom of his father's words. His father had not bound his hand to the soil, but his hand to his heart. Now, wherever he thrusts his hand, he finds his heart--and his father.

❦ ❦ ❦

I am no 'Pollyanna' who insists that there is a silver lining in every storm cloud. There's a lot of wind and rain in some of those clouds. I have watched the driving hail strip the growing corn down to the naked stalk and walked amidst the havoc wrought by the savage wind unleashed upon the golden grain. I have swallowed hard and suffered in silence when forced to accept less than I thought I deserved. There have been times when my own foolishness, or carelessness, rose up to mock me and demand the 'pound of flesh' which never satisfied the ravenous hunger of shame. I too have grieved the death of youthful dreams, have bid farewell to unfulfilled ambitions, and kept my promise when doing so closed other doors which offered fulfillment of what was desired above all.

These experiences are not unknown to persons who are the possessors of happiness. Happy are those who have the strength to bear weakness, who have the courage to face their fears, and whose embrace of life enlarges through every loss.

❦ ❦ ❦

I peer at the black and white pictures, now yellowing with age, taken by my parents during those early years, and gaze with curiosity and wonder at the child I see that bears my name. Even these pictures stir no memory. All of those delicious, terrifying, comforting, exciting, tastes, sounds, smells and touches lie buried in some inaccessible vault while I still search for the key. I remember the smell of tobacco smoke in my father's clothes, and the comforting feel of his work-worn hands as a boy of six, but not of his tender touch and soft voice when he played with me as a toddler learning to walk. Is it a blessing or a tragedy that we do not remember the experiences of our early childhood?

༄ ༄ ༄

Happiness is not the gentle stroke of good luck, nor is it the sensuous power of success. Good luck sets us up for the sucker punch of a blow to the solar plexus at the moment we have raised our hands above our heads in praise to the gods of fortune and fame. Success is a miserable companion on the way to the top and a fair-weather friend on the way down.

༄ ༄ ༄

The Japanese Haiku probed my heart with particular poignancy:
>Seeing my birth-cord
>>kept at our old
>>native place...
>New Year's day I wept.

Whence these tears? For the security of childhood too long forgotten? Or for the tragedy of being born? It could well be both, for tears are never simple things nor life an open book.

I do know this. We spend the greater part of early life attempting to throw off the cocoon of birth and adolescence. There is an unreasonable urge to escape the influence and structures of our nativity, longing for the bright wings of individuality and unhindered self-expression. I fear that our age has made this urge a privilege, if not a demand. With dispassionate skill, the therapist enters in to probe the agonizing core of one's being until the new self emerges, freed from the traumas of parental love gone awry. Healing from old wounds is necessary, but where is the birth-cord?

The stewardship of life is a gift to us, and if we have despised this birthright, we would do well to weep for the birth-cord of our nativity. These are good tears.

We always know more than we can tell. There is a knowledge at the core of the self for which we will never find words. It rises up within us without our bidding and cannot be forgotten or erased by the most strenuous act of the will nor by the most delirious ecstasy of emotion.

In the bond of love and attachment experienced by the first man and woman, each has a knowledge of the absence of the other. In the pleasure of life's most gratifying moments, there is a knowledge of the passing away of that life, and that is death. In the most self-assured managing of one's possessions in life, there is the knowledge of their impending loss.

❦ ❦ ❦

He cradled the rifle in his arms, on a cold winter morning. Suddenly a red fox, surprised by his silent approach, froze in fear. Crouching only a short distance away beside a snow covered shock of corn, the fox stared into his eyes with a fear that he came to understand as that which bound him to the creature, for that brief moment in time. Only when he finally shuffled his feet did the animal release him from the compelling power of that common knowledge and bounded away. The gun was never raised; his aim was no longer to kill.

❦ ❦ ❦

If there are two sides to humanity, Jesus will often be found on the wrong side. This is a scandal to the righteous, but pleasing to God.

❦ ❦ ❦

There are flowers that bloom near every tomb. And if it seems strange that life should flaunt its color so close to darkness, then one has missed both the sense of death and the secret of life. To the one who observes, earth promises us more than it takes from us. That our destiny on earth is in the dust from which we came cannot be doubted. It is only the spirit in us that fears the darkness. The power of the soil to produce life out of death is a parable of hope to the human heart. Yet, hope soon stumbles over its own ignorance and with Job, whispers the doubt that follows every soul, "If a man dies shall he live again?"

The flowers of a thousand generations have never opened a tomb nor lighted its darkness into life. These are only feeble intimations of a stillborn truth. The odor of death is scarcely masked by the fragrance of life--flowers bloom outside of the tomb, not within it. Let flowers bloom close to every tomb. And if it seems strange that life should be so bold in death, then remember, there is one tomb with living flowers in it.

I go there occasionally to smell its fragrance.

༄ ༄ ༄

"They heard the sound of the Lord God walking in the garden at the time of the evening breeze" (Genesis 3:8).

It is a lonely garden that has fragrance without sound. The esthetic thrill of well-kept borders guarding exotic plants soon gives way to a longing for friendly footsteps anticipating response. Those who make beauty their divinity shall be haunted by inescapable silence. It is easier to clothe ourselves in the familiarity of the daily routine than to acknowledge the sound of divinity leading the heart into new echoes of response. We disguise ourselves behind the facade of friendliness and scarcely permit the intimacy of friendship to become a spiritual reality. It is more comfortable to talk of theology than faith; safer to make small talk than reveal deep feelings.

The voice of God always speaks our name and that is how we recognize the sound of divinity.

☙ ☙ ☙

"If you and daddy die, then we will only need two placemats at our table," the 5 year old said to his mother. Two placemats, one for him and one for his brother. A visual image used to tame the terror of an unspeakable fear. Who will care for us? This is the question we dare not ask, but can never forget.

☙ ☙ ☙

"Teacher, I brought you my son; he has a spirit that makes him unable to speak" (Mark 9:17). The distressed father who brought his afflicted son to Jesus for healing identified the boy's malady as having an "inarticulate spirit." The older translations called it a "dumb spirit."

"How long has he had this?" asked Jesus. "From childhood," replied the father. "It has often cast him into the fire and to the water, to destroy him... if you are able... help us."

From childhood. Of course! Here is where our tentative movements into relationships are sometimes stillborn, and we withdraw into the security of acting out our life rather than experiencing it. This is why we can move with facility in a technical world that is satisfied with proficiency, and care little that we so often appear to have a "dumb spirit"--or care even less that others appear to be speaking without making sounds.

Absorbed in the mechanics of living, the windows of the self become steamed over with our daily breath--we cannot see out, nor others in. Bound with inhibitions we take refuge in a vocabulary of vacuities. Where there are no conversations from the heart there are often convulsions of the spirit. In our inarticulate rage, we flail and flounder, falling into the fire and the water. Wordlessly, the rescue continues its relentless cycle. Despair is dumb but dutiful. Is a cure possible?

The strange voice we hear is our own. The barrenness of busyness forces the heart to protest its exclusion from the reality of relationship. Estrangement is an aching abyss that lies unresponsive to the ministrations of bright immediacies. Despair is akin to faith, and feeling to being. Compelled from within, the mind dares to ask the question for which the heart has long sought an answer--If you are able!"

I would like to have heard the boy speak.

※ ※ ※

Whether one speaks **in** a tongue or speaks **with** a tongue, I cannot help but agree with Paul who said, "I would rather speak five words with my mind, in order to instruct others also, than ten thousand words in a tongue" (1 Corinthians 14:19). One of the great truths of redemptive love is the inspiration of the human mind by the action of the Spirit of God. Paul intimates that we can "think the thoughts of God" through the prompting of the personality by the Spirit of God (1 Corinthians 2:11-12).

༺ ༺ ༺

I have often been accused of being a maverick and a non-conformist. On the cattle range, a maverick is a calf whose mother has died and who must go from cow to cow to steal a little milk in order to survive. The maverick must be discretely promiscuous and not adverse to taking some punishment. As it turns out, the maverick ends up being stronger and healthier than the others because of an unlimited supply and a robust appetite. I don't mind being called a maverick!

> " In a world of fugitives
> One who moves in the opposite direction
> Will appear to run away."
> [J. G. Hamann]

༺ ༺ ༺

One definition of the grace of God says that it is 'unmerited favor.' That is true, but it tends to focus on our undeservedness. To receive as a gift what we have not earned is truly a blessing of grace and an expression of love. At the same time, because grace has its source in love, what love promises when it makes the other an object of love **creates** in the loved one an expectation of a blessing. We have not merited this blessing, but it is rightfully ours because it has been promised by love.

❦ ❦ ❦

Those who protest the stretching of the mind through the communication of the gospel, and insist that one must speak "simply" like Jesus did, find no justification for this intellectual barrenness in Scripture. Jesus constantly prefaced his teaching with the challenge "What do you think?" There is a temptation to probe the complacency of those who sit week after week in church under the preaching of the Word with the question, "What do you use your brain for?" And yet, perhaps those who listen would like the courage to ask the same question of those of us who speak the Word of God!

❦ ❦ ❦

Fear is like fatigue. When the muscle is able to relax, the fatigue disappears. The self is like a muscle. It contracts and reacts to stimulation through feeling. The feeling does not go anywhere when the fear disappears. Rather, the feeling releases its grip on the fear and "lets go." This is why feeling itself is capable of restoration and recovery when negative and painful sensations are replaced by positive and supportive ones.

❦ ❦ ❦

My father used to plant potatoes every Spring. First we would cut them into pieces, making sure that each piece had an "eye" in it, as he called it. From this "eye" a sprout would form and then the pieces were ready to be placed in the ground. One thing remained, however, before we could plant. To ensure a good harvest of potatoes, my father said, we must plant them when the moon is full. So we would wait until the propitious time, and then place them in the ground.

We always had sufficient potatoes, come fall, as I recall. In those days, I did not venture to submit this folk wisdom to a scientific test by deliberately planting some during another phase of the moon. I doubt that he did either. It was probably the only superstition that I recall my father ever including in his otherwise common sense approach to the tilling of the soil and the husbandry of our livestock.

Even as I write this, why do I feel a sense of uneasiness in making such a clear distinction between superstition and common sense? He would not have been happy with such a charge. For him, the working of the soil was a participation in a cycle of sowing and reaping, suffering crop failures and rejoicing at bountiful harvests. He never disclosed his inner feelings, neither of grief at his losses nor joy at his successes. I gather now that he lived a self-life in communion with the seasons of nature, with the rhythm of birth, life and death and, yes, by the phases of the moon! This may be the most common of all senses!

༺ ༺ ༺

Our deepest feelings are often invested in that which has the capacity to break our hearts. At the same time, it is necessary to make these risky investments in order to plant the seed of love in the soil of life. The risk of failure is no reason not to go forth and plant.

༺ ༺ ༺

Jesus said, "Where your treasure is, there will your heart be also (Matthew 6:21). Would we be wrong in reversing it and say--where your heart is, there will your treasure be also? He did counsel a rich man to "sell what you have and give to the poor, and you will have treasure in heaven" (Matthew 19:21). He did insist by parable that the uninvested talent be taken from the one and given to the other who had multiplied his through use (Matthew 25).

The increasing complaint that life is empty and unrewarding cannot be justified by circumstances alone. The answer is unmistakable, even if unpalatable-- we each must be the major investors in our own life. The depressed are robbers of temples--expecting to gain what they do not give. The chronic complainers are misers--demanding room service without paying the bill. The skeptics are misanthropes--scanning the horizon of humanity with distorted lens. The bored are parasites--waiting for the inspiration of others to provide a vicarious thrill.

⁂ ⁂ ⁂

I do not believe that Jesus Christ is the answer to a "God-shaped vacuum" in the human heart, as a philospher once put it. This is a nice text for a sophomore in a christian college who is searching for an intellectual argument for the experience of God. The problem with a vacuum is that it is indiscriminate and will draw in anything that is floating around in the air.

I am more attracted to the wisdom of Michael Polanyi who once wrote, "Our Believing is conditioned at its source by our belonging." Psychologists tell us that forming early attachments, called bonding, is an essential basis for healthy and effective personal relationships in life. Jesus said, "where two or three are gathered in my name, I am there among them" (Matt 18:20). I grew up with a strong sense of belonging. I have never had trouble believing.

⁂ ⁂ ⁂

We are each born with a deficit of love. We are deprived at the core of our being of the original blessing, and make impossible demands upon ourselves for fulfillment. This 'original sin' traps every person in the vicious circle of non-fulfillment. Despite every effort to make up for the deficit in the self through knowledge and awareness, we still find that we are prone to using and abusing others.

Some, meaning to save us from this condition,

tell us that we are worthless, not merely hopeless. Only by denying ourselves, we are warned, can we be accepted by God's grace. We have no merit in ourselves, and no right to expect anything of God, so the evangelists tell us. This 'half-truth' of the gospel of grace can offer the gift of salvation, but ordinarily does not result in the full truth of being blessed! Look around, the church is filled with people who profess God's salvation from sin but are still searching for God's blessing of love. Not having received the blessing promised, many Christians still are looking for the 'pay-off' in serving God.

※ ※ ※

Fleeing from King Saul, lonely and isolated, "David said longingly, 'O that someone would give me water to drink from the well of Bethlehem that is by the gate.'" Three of David's 'mighty men,' hearing him speak, broke through the camp of the Philistines, drew water from the well in Bethlehem and brought it to David. "But he would not drink of it; he poured it out to the Lord, for he said, 'The Lord forbid that I should do this. Can I drink of the blood of the men who went at the risk of their lives?' Therefore he would not drink of it" (2 Samuel 23:13-17).

How many times have we sent people back to the well in Bethlehem in a misguided attempt to make us happy? How often have we drunk the water to satisfy a craving only to miss the blessing of a caring heart! We exchange the priceless longing for self fulfillment for the cheap currency of emotional needs. But the inflationary spiral of needs propels us into emotional bankruptcy, and we file for 'chapter 11' by retaining the services of a therapist. And if the therapist is wise, she will become a liturgist and, instead of handing us the water to drink, will empower us to pour it out 'to the Lord,' and thereby receive the blessing. We can teach therapists and counselors the skill of finding the well at Bethlehem, but the wisdom of knowing what to do with it when it is found, is an art known only to those who themselves know the blessing. When longing is fulfilled by love, it is strange how needs diminish.

⁂ ⁂ ⁂

The justice of God does not require the suspension of grace, despite what some moralists say. In the final judgment, God may give the parents of the man who murdered both his father and his mother permission to decide his eternal fate. If they should seek reconciliation rather than retaliation, who will claim that an injustice has been done?

⁂ ⁂ ⁂

God does not duck and dodge the reality of evil, attributing it to human sin and blaming it on the Devil. God is the author of the drama, in which pain and pleasure, suffering and joy, good and evil are part of the plot.

Faith means that we as human participants in

that drama have the revelation of God himself. He is the author who encompasses the beginning and the end and is himself participating in the drama even as we live it out. God takes full responsibility. This, at least, is a start.

❦ ❦ ❦

Jesus played no favorites!

He ignored the categories established within his own society. For him the despised Samaritan was a woman who could give <u>him</u> a drink, the self righteous Pharisee a man who wanted to talk, the leper a person who needed to be touched.

While people came to him in bunches, needs came with a name. A congregation was not a mob to send home to eat, but individuals to be fed with bread broken with his own hands. In a crowd he was never simply pushed by people, but touched by someone who hurt. Within the shouting sounds of a multitude he heard the cry of the blind man, the sigh of a sinner, the murmur of a skeptic. He let people be like who they were and offered to help them become who could be. He had no uniforms for his disciples and no masks for his friends. He did not ask for conformity but for commitment. His style was love, his pattern devotion.

❦ ❦ ❦

A joyless life is one that has lost its sense of wonder. Our sense of wonder is lost when our curiosity becomes clinical. We have an insatiable desire to explore, picking apart life like a young child so fascinated with how a toy works that he cannot resist taking it apart. Alas, he has discovered its secret but lost the joy of playing with it.

When our curiosity becomes too clinical the wonder is lost in life. It's bad enough when we become clinical about the way we feel, about the way we live, but when we become clinical about who we are and what the meaning of life is, we have passed out of the sanctuary into the laboratory.

We lose our sense of wonder when worship becomes self-analysis. The divine image in us is meant to be a lens through which we can discover the reality of God as well as the mystery of our own being, not a mirror in which we probe the secrets of our past. Worship is meant to be something that is directed away from us toward one who is our counterpart in every way, and yet stands outside of the boundaries of our human finitude and weakness.

Our sense of wonder is lost when the miraculous becomes routine. When the science of human behavior destroys the mythical life of the soul, life is sanitized of all sacredness. When the star which the wise men followed becomes a comet explained in an astronomy textbook, we have been given information but not inspiration.

෴ ෴ ෴

His name is Brogan. He is twenty months old, and he is my grandson. We play in the park, feed the ducks, and pretend that he is running away and I can barely run fast enough to catch him. He calls me Papa, and for just a brief moment looks into my eyes with undisguised love and trust. It was, for me at least, and I think for him, an experience that psychologists call bonding. Like two gulls swooping across a sunlit meadow, our winged souls touched in flight. We both sensed the presence of the other and felt the sudden stab of recognition that yields a pleasure almost too painful to bear.

Then it struck me. He will not remember this moment nor hold for long the image of my face in his mind. For a few weeks perhaps, aided by a picture and some parental prompting, he will give the correct answer when quizzed about name and face.

When we meet again I will enter his familiar world as a stranger and we will need to become friends once again. Yes I know, the bonding may well be there, the psychologists tell me. But I want Brogan to tell me! I want him to remember, not just my face, but his own feelings of shared joy and love. When he is older, I will tell him the story, of course, and he will believe it. But he will not likely ever recover the feelings that became so much a part of the self that he now recognizes as his own. When he awakens to himself, like all of us, he will ponder the mystery of those years between his birth and his awakening. Part of the self remains silent and never speaks, no matter how fluent the vocabulary of the mind.

❧ ❧ ❧

We are easy prey for the comfort of convenience. The challenge to follow Christ is felt by many to be an invasion of personal freedom. The imperative of Christian ministry becomes an interruption of the indispensable routine. It is unfortunate, but true, that the highest motivation among Christians often is the opportunity which is made the most convenient. Not the least of Jesus' sufferings was the "inconvenience of the cross."

I protest the comfort of complacency that editorializes profoundly on distant atrocities, while the crippled crawl beneath the closed Windows of compassion. Jesus wept over Jerusalem, not Rome. He followed his tears into the streets where others knew his discomfort. Strangely, in his distress, the hope of humanity recognized the heart of God--and they were not wrong.

❧ ❧ ❧

Those who lack the virtue of generosity suffer a spiritual deficit. Their own spirit is cramped and crushed, like an eagle caged in a zoo. Lacking the freedom to soar its spirit turns sour and surly. Stalking the boundaries of its limited existence, the fettered spirit misinterprets the freedom of others as prodigality, and becomes miserly and mean. It is the meanness of spirit, not the habit of miserliness that marks the spiritual deficit in the ungenerous.

Fearing the bonding of spirit with another as a form of bondage, those who lack the spirit of generosity retaliate when they are wounded and are impatient with the suffering of others. The ungenerous spirit maintains its freedom from the demands of others by cutting the cords of human compassion and declaring resident alien status in the human family.

※ ※ ※

Friendship may be the only form of human social relationships which is sustained primarily by kindness.

Kindness is the glue which binds friends together. If I should humiliate a friend, be insensitive to the feelings of a friend, cause unnecessary harm or hurt to a friend, or in any way treat a friend as an object that I use for my own pleasure and gratification, the friendship dissolves. There is no reason why a person should want to continue a friendship where there is no kindness, other than we use another to meet other needs. And in that case it is not a true and healthy friendship.

Kindness is the seed we plant in another's garden to grow fruit for our own enjoyment. When we care for the garden of another's life we are ensuring a harvest of fruit for our own pleasure. The proverb says it well: "Those who are kind reward themselves, but the cruel do themselves harm" (Proverbs 11:17).

※ ※ ※

Why does it seem easier to show kindness to a friend than to one's marriage partner? When persons who are married do not show kindness as a consistent pattern, the marriage is no longer a caring and loving one. Such a marriage has failed the litmus test of love. For love is not a relation where one only takes care **of** the other, but where both take care **for** the other. When one becomes incapacitated and unable to care for oneself, taking care of the other become the deepest expression of love. The promise of love includes the commitment to the care of each other should the need arise. But mutual care for each other is what keeps lovers friends and produces the fruit of kindness.

※ ※ ※

Intimacy is the intensification of otherness.

The awareness of the **self** of the other as absolutely standing over and against our own self is like an electric shock. The experiences shared which seemed to draw two people together as having 'something in common,' now reveal a confrontation with the mystery and spirit of another self which is totally other than one's own self. The shared intimacy of communication and communion intensifies the **otherness** of each.

❧ ❧ ❧

Writing to his friend from a prison cell, Dietrich Bonhoeffer, the German pastor and theologian reflected upon a quotation from Girodano Bruno that stuck in his mind: "There can be something frightening about the sight of a friend; no enemy can be so terrifying as he." Bonhoeffer added: "Does 'terrifying' refer to the inherent danger of betrayal, inseparable from close intimacy. . . ?" There is indeed something 'terrifying' as well as exhilarating about the encounter with another whose spirit is open to ours. When this moment of vulnerability and exposure to the spirit of another occurs, it is an unavoidable experience of intimacy. We are not often prepared for it and shrink from its implications. But this retreat from intimacy dissolves the other into a safe, but distant, counterpart to ourselves.

❧ ❧ ❧

The human spirit is the core of the self as desiring, cherishing, longing, and believing. As we grow and develop as persons, our spirit selects and assimilates from all of our experiences; it creates and colors life with the tension and texture which vibrates with urgency and reposes in peace. The spirit wills and resists, it opens and closes, it gives and receives. To share our spirit is to receive the other into the sacred shrine of what is most personal and dear; to share the spirit of the other is to be welcomed freely and trustingly into their holy of holies.

※ ※ ※

    Children are not born with courage because they have not yet learned fear. Fearlessness is the armor which shame wears when it goes forth to seize another prize to exhibit in the inner room called despair. Every encounter must be a conquest, and every lover a trophy. Each time that shame is felt over the price one must pay to bring love to the side of fear, the armor of fearlessness is quickly assumed. When love attempts to cast out the hidden fear and heal the shame, it is love that is cast out, fear remains. These people are brave and beautiful, in their own eyes. They are pictures of sadness and sorrow for those who love and lament.
    Fearlessness is not the absence of fear. Fearlessness is fear in its full dress uniform seeking a parade and a prize. In attempting to be fearless, one seeks to overcome fear by feeding it with the illusion of power and invulnerability.
    Courage is more humble and far more realistic. It accepts fear as a necessary part of life. Without courage, fear would never permit us to open the door to life and love. It takes courage to hope and to have faith when we know fear. It takes courage to live with our weaknesses, our vulnerability, our loneliness. It takes courage to live with fear.

※ ※ ※

    Compassion is only a feeling until it becomes an act of mercy. In showing mercy, one seeks to alleviate pain, temper justice, and restore relationships. While mercy is prompted by compassion, it has its source in the moral virtue of promoting the value of a human life when it least deserves it or cannot bear it. We applaud acts of mercy because we recognize the moral goodness of such actions which go beyond the legal demands of the law.

※ ※ ※

The brokenness of the human spirit is a deeper and more creative edge than guilt and remorse for sin. A sense of guilt is not creative and produces no positive motivation toward spiritual wholeness. We tend to forget that the cross of Christ only has significance as a place where sin is judged for those who have experienced the power of resurrection and the gift of the Spirit of God.

※ ※ ※

Jesus was not only raised from the grave; he was raised from hell. In the deepest caverns of the abyss, there is the sign of the cross. and it is empty.

※ ※ ※

The cemetary adjoining my boyhood farm was separated from us by only a wire fence through which I easily could crawl back and forth. Having crossed over many times in my youthful play, I shall not be surprised to find myself crossing once more--for the last time--drawn by the view from the other side.

୨⋒୨ ୨⋒୨ ୨⋒୨

Love is intrinsically tragic. Who dares to love must be prepared to embrace the tragic for the sake of holding fast that which is loved.

The essence of the tragic is a collision between two or more values in real life where no single answer is the right one. The moral issues in life are layered and complex. Choices sometimes have to be made, and failure to act due to moral uncertainty may itself constitute betrayal of the human bond that unites us. The compassionate person is prepared to enter into the arena of the tragic for the sake of upholding human life in situations where the simple good is not possible. The moralist avoids the tragic by taking a stand for moral principle as having priority over real life choices.

୨⋒୨ ୨⋒୨ ୨⋒୨

Dietrich Bonhoeffer, who left the security of his office as a German pastor to enter the conspiracy against Hitler, once said, "What is worse than doing evil is being evil. It is worse for a liar to tell the truth than of a lover of truth to lie."

The lover of truth is basically an honest person who has demonstrated a consistent pattern of truthfulness in word and deed. The liar is basically a dishonest person who will use the truth to deceive and manipulate others.

When evil appears in the form of truth, we are

blinded to its moral danger because we ordinarily assume that behind true words is an honest person. This is why it is worse for a liar to tell the truth. The liar counts on our commitment to take a person at his or her word until proven otherwise. By that time, it is too late. The liar has deceived us by telling the truth and gaining this advantage over us.

When an honest person, for one reason or another, is caught in a lie, we immediately note the contradiction because we know the person to be basically honest in word and deed. When the lie is acknowledged and forgiveness sought, the virtue of honesty remains intact despite the lapse. If deception becomes a pattern and the telling of lies flagrant, then we would finally revise our judgment of the person's character because the virtue of honesty no longer is evident.

If an evil person deceives us by using truth as a tactic for gaining our trust so as to do us harm, the act of deception reveals a basically dishonest person. We are more vulnerable to evil disguised as truth because in such a person there is no virtue of honesty to which we can appeal in looking for repentance and recompense.

The measure of strength as a virtue of character is not how much pressure one can exert against others but how much stress one can absorb without breaking apart. The strong person is not impervious to pain but persevering in purpose.

⚜ ⚜ ⚜

Serenity results from spiritual perception and spiritual counsel as the wisdom of God's Word and Spirit. Spiritual counsel gives vision, clarity, hope and healing to the self amidst conflict and confusion.

Serenity is not a feeling that comes by detaching oneself from inner conflicts and external threat. Nor is serenity achieved by seeking to escape from the ordinary into a state of extraordinary peace. Serenity is spiritual perception which integrates the extraordinary into the ordinary. When the vision of a larger purpose and meaning to life is brought into one's concrete situation and experience, a new picture comes into focus. Serenity is spiritual counsel which one receives into the soul as a deeper wisdom, such that a new capacity to grasp the whole of reality emerges. When spiritual perception and spiritual counsel do their work, spiritual healing results and the gift of serenity is received.

⚜ ⚜ ⚜

I live with the certainty of my own death. My death, I suppose, will be a loss for those who love me, and I can even speak of it as a loss of my own life. But it can never be a defeat. I am not in a "life-and-death" struggle, in which death can rob me of some hoped-for victory or prize.

༺ ༺ ༺

We do not use language, language uses us, wrote Heidegger. Being comes to us, he said, not through the words alone, but through the spaces which words create. Too often we close these spaces with the cement of logic so that no meaning can leak out. In doing so, we are plastering the inside of our own tomb.

༺ ༺ ༺

The love that God expresses can be tough as well as tender.

God's love has clear expectations which are realistic as well as purposeful. God's love is not a rushing torrent that devastates all in its path. Nor is God's love naive and idealistic, blind to the realities and complexities of life. Like God's love, human love is realistic and resourceful, but has its practical limits. One does not "simply" love and expect everything to work out. That is simplistic sentimentality.

Tough love is not brutal and unfeeling. It's toughness is not the absence of tenderness, but the practical realism of its expectations. Love has realistic expectations as to the yield on its investment. It also sets realistic criteria for measuring the goals it attempts to produce. The portfolio of love is set for high yield but low risk. The personal investment is total, but the expectations are in proportion to the growth potential.

❦ ❦ ❦

Faith is not the bridge we build to get to God--that is folly!--but it is creating a path for God to come to us.

Faith and folly are sibling rivals, growing up in the same household, but not cut out of the same cloth. Folly may be likened to the weeds which grow amidst the wheat, appearing at early stages to be quite similar. It is only at harvest, said Jesus, that the wheat can be separated as it has produced a full head of grain (Matthew 13:24-30).

Folly, has two step sisters, greed and grandiosity. Grandiosity, psychologists tell us, is the illusion that one is greater than one really is, leading to delusions of self importance and success. Greed, of course, is the insatiable desire to accumulate things for the sake of gaining power and security.

Folly manufactures evidence where there is none, while faith sees evidence that is not visible. Folly is the attempt to "make visible" what is unreal and so elicit commitment from others and give oneself permission to satisfy greed and grandiosity. Faith envisions what is real, though not visible, while folly makes visible what is unreal.

❦ ❦ ❦

Love is not a torrent of water unleashed down the side of a mountain, but Love is a steady flow of water through a channel which irrigates a field. The river which graces the land with life-sustaining water becomes a devastating and destructive force when it overflows its boundaries. What makes a river is not the passivity of its current, but that its passion is kept within bounds.

Love without passion is anemic and sterile. The famous Dead Sea in Palestine is so called because it has no outlet. Eventually the salts and minerals in the water make it inhospitable for living organisms. When love dies and loses its passion it not only becomes sterile but toxic.

※ ※ ※

The love of God is portrayed as well by God's passionate anger as well as by his solicitous and searching care. God's passionate love is like a fierce warrior who has righteous anger at that which demeans or destroys the object of love. But the passion in that anger is well aimed and not merely well armed. Its aim is accurate and its focus is narrow and laser-like in its clean and cutting edge.

Where the passion of love is without the boundary of purpose it becomes indiscriminate, promiscuous and fatal. The passion of love can produce giddiness as well as gladness. Love that rides the crest of passion's wave becomes merely "high surf," and we must remember that waves reach their crest only when they are about to crash on shore.

❦ ❦ ❦

The grace of God must first kill before it can make alive. It was the barrenness of Sarah, not the virility of Abraham, that produced the promised seed. When we forget that, there is an Ishmael that cannot be comforted and an Esau who weeps to no avail.

❦ ❦ ❦

We should not be surpised by death, even when it comes when we don't expect it. As tragic as it may seem--and all deaths are a grevious loss--death is woven into the very fabric of life.

Holding my father's hands and feeling his last heart beat as his life slipped away, I realized that these were the hands that had held my newborn life and felt the pulse of my heart at birth. There is a time when hearts begin to beat, and there is a time when they stop. So begins and ends our allotted time on earth.

❦ ❦ ❦

Hope requires risk, so much that it creates expectations beyond our reach. Hope makes us vulnerable to future and even greater loss. Hope exposes us to disappointment, frustration and betrayal. Faith plants the seed and promises a harvest, and so creates hope. But with the promise of a harvest comes the possibility that the promise will fail. That is the betrayal that hope must bear. Without faith as the investment of one's precious life and resources in the power of life, the burden of hope could not be borne. But faith bears that burden in partnership with hope, for it is partnership with God, the author and creator of life.

✥ ✥ ✥

Why is it that betrayal seems to be a failure that is so fatal?

I saw it printed in block letters with a blue felt tip pen across the top of the mirror in the men's restroom in a restaurant in San Francisco: **JUDAS COME HOME--ALL IS FORGIVEN!**

Could it be true? Would even Judas, the betrayer of Jesus, have found forgiveness if he had sought out the very one whom he had betrayed? Can God forgive anything and everything? Or, does this bit of theological graffiti press beyond the limits of even divine love and grace?

We know that Judas was stricken with guilt and shame after having betrayed Jesus. Though he admitted his guilt and returned the money he had been paid to betray Jesus, he did not find forgiveness from others nor in himself. The darkness of despair closed in upon him--a night where there was no gentleness to provide healing and hope.

Judas reminds us that to love others and to make promises to others is to risk betrayal. Even as we point to the betrayal of others, we know that the seeds of betrayal lie hidden in our own best intentions.

Betrayal is felt to be an unforgivable act because

it exposes ambivalence at the deepest core of human relationships. When we cannot trust our own trust, and dare not be loyal to loyalty, we feel the cords that bind together our deepest and most precious moments slip out of our grasp. Perhaps this is why, if a Devil did not exist, we would need to invent one. The defection of what once was good to become evil cries out for explanation. We can let neither God nor humankind bear the burden of introducing evil into what we all want to believe is essentially good.

Why is it that a single act of betrayal can destroy all of one's life? What is betrayal such a devastating failure that it has the power to condemn the past and contaminate the future? Why, for some, as in the case of Judas, does suicide appear to be the only personal atonement for betrayal?

The act of the betrayer not only contains the power to destroy a relationship, it tears at the very fabric of human society. The very concept of betrayal is grounded in a structure of community based on loyalty, trust and commitment. A lie is not betrayal until it destroys the bond of friendship. 'It is not the fact that you lied to me that is so terrible,' Nietszche once said, 'but the fact that I can no longer trust you.' Betrayal does more than deceive, it destroys trust in those who are deceived.

The other disciples certainly failed Jesus as well. Peter denied Jesus three times during the crucial hours of his trial. Without the resurrection of the crucified Jesus, there would have been no power of forgiveness in the cross. Without a deep personal encounter with the living Christ following the resurrection, the disciples would not have experienced forgiveness and healing of their shame.

But what of Judas? And what of each one of us who harbor secret shame and long for a reassuring word from Jesus?

Can we as children close doors that defy our attempts to open them as adults? I think so. I have them. I know they're there. Some of these doors are to keep me out rather than close me in. I no longer remember why they were closed, but only that they must be opened. Behind some doors lie undiscovered and unrevealed shame; behind others the bones of a child, who bears my name, buried in secret in order that the adult should live. These doors must opened and the child healed and led forth into life.

ᘛ ᘛ ᘛ

As I grow toward health and wholeness, I believe that the resurrected Jesus will explore with me the still unopened doors and dispel unknown fears. He will give life to youthful dreams that perished in the anguish of failure, and release the child within to become the health of my older years. Not all doors can be opened at once. And so I live with rooms not yet invaded by his presence, for I also have spacious rooms that open outward toward the green prairies and undulating hills. And there are people in this landscape, moving toward me, and I am not afraid.

EPILOGUE

Judas Come Home, All is Forgiven

When Judas, his betrayer, saw that Jesus was condemned, he repented and brought back the thirty pieces of silver to the chief priests and the elders. He said, "I have sinned by betraying innocent blood." But they said, "What is that to us? See to it yourself." Throwing down the pieces of silver in the temple, he departed; and he went and hanged himself (Matthew 27:3-5).

The Morning After

The confrontation between Jesus and Judas occurs in the very place which Judas chose to take his own life. The cold wind of death is stilled; the howling of hell silenced. Satan is held at bay. The power of darkness retreats in the presence of the glorious light and life of the risen Lord. The relentless logic of despair within the mind of Judas is made foolish by the sudden appearance of Jesus in the lonely place to which Judas retreated for his own final act upon this earth.

Judas is stunned, but not speechless. The skin on his neck is bruised from the rasping pull of the rope which jerked his head to the side. His throat is raw and hoarse from the shrieks of despair he threw out into the night as he plunged into the darkness. He involuntarily jerks his arm away from the touch of Jesus. He will not be comforted With a choking sensation he feels anger welling up, its urgency giving way to words.

Why have you come to torment me? Aren't you satisfied that I perished from this earth by my own hands? Leave me alone, Jesus of Nazareth, let me go to the hell I deserve. I betrayed you, and delivered you over to your own death. I said I was sorry, but sorry isn't enough. Sorrow doesn't change anything.

You are right, Judas Iscariot. There are things that do not change. Though I am not one who causes torment.

Yes, that's true. I brought the torment on myself, and you by failing your trust in me and causing your death. Yet you do torment me. You will probably tell me that you still love me, and so gain virtue for yourself and add another millstone around my neck. Don't you realize that for the betrayer love is a cruel reminder of failure? Go away! I have enough pain without your love punishing me further.

I tell you that you love me, and that is the cause of your pain and torment.

You're talking nonsense. If I loved you I would not have betrayed you. After all, betrayal, is not an act of love, its an act of treachery. You can't deny the logic of that.

Judas, betrayal is the sin of love against love. Unlike other sins, betrayal uses love to destroy what is loved. This is why betrayal does not end a relationship, why you cannot put an end to our relationship by yourself. Forgiveness for the act of betrayal seems impossible if betrayal is the final act. Yet betrayal is not the end of love. You hate yourself because you love me. You betrayed me because you love me.

For me, betrayal was a single, final, and fatal act. An aberration in myself for which I can find no cause. I expected you to speak of your love for me, but not of mine for you. What you're saying makes no sense to me.

How can you stand there and say that I love you? How could this love be the cause of my torment and the source of my betrayal? You chose me--I didn't choose you. You called me to be your disciple!

In that you are correct. Judas, I chose you because you were given to me by my Father in heaven.

Oh, so I really had no choice! It was all a divine plan and I was one of the pawns on your Father's game board! I resent that implication. For my part, I sensed an opportunity to fulfill my desire to serve God through the bringing in of his Kingdom.

Such strong desire to serve God has been called love.

Don't twist my words Jesus! I became your disciple because I thought we had the same goal--to recover our land from the Romans and establish God's Kingdom of righteousness and holiness. After your baptism I heard you speak openly of the coming of the Kingdom. Many of us heard the same words from you.

I came not only with words, but the Spirit of God was upon me, performing signs and wonders of healing the sick and feeding the hungry. Were you not drawn to me along with the others by the power of my Father who loves the world?

You say drawn, I say seduced--by a power I didn't quite understand. And that sealed my destiny here on earth. Except for you I'd have been living a quite ordinary life, with my fanatical zeal partially tamed by unsuccessful ventures of political resistance. My friends and I would be sharing our dreams and telling our stories. But when you called me to be a disciple I risked everything on that--and failed.

I understand failure. The other disciples failed as well-- they were scattered like sheep without a shepherd. I was left alone. You had each other, even in your failure.

Do you know that I went to them after betraying you and begged their forgiveness? They said that the devil had entered into me. They blamed me for everything. When I became your disciple, I began a friendship that turned out to be fatal for both of us. How can anyone call that love?
Tell me, Jesus of Nazareth--how did you decide to call me as one of the twelve? You say you chose me because your Father in heaven gave me to you. But why we twelve out of the many? Why me?

There was a decision to be made. I turned to the Father in prayer for guidance.

Are you telling me that I, Judas Iscariot, the man who betrayed you, am an answer to prayer! Do you still believe in prayer?

I did not pray so that every decision might be to my advantage, but so that I might love every decision as affirmed by the Father who loves me. You are indeed an answer to my prayer; that is why I loved you and washed your feet on the very night that you betrayed me.

You knew even then, did you not, that I was plotting to betray you? Why didn't you stop me, or at least expose me as a traitor?

I knew, but I sought your love for me by sharing my love for you. I have prayed for you, Judas, that your love might return and that you might be healed.

I once prayed too. But no answers came. If I cannot love and cannot pray, what hope is there? I'm confused. You tell me that I'm an answer to prayer and that you've prayed for me to be healed. But I sealed my fate with my fatal act of betrayal. Death was the final act of mercy which delivered my soul from the torment of life. I feel nothing, neither love nor hope.

How is it, Judas, that you feel such anger at me if you have killed all feeling?

Because you bring back to me all that I died to get away from. I closed the door to my life and sealed it with my own death. But now you've opened that door again. You have awakened all of the old feelings, but none that are new.

God is not the God of the dead, Judas, but of the living. Because I live, you also shall live.

Yes, I remember that you taught us that. But that had reference to Abraham, Isaac, and Jacob, who all died in faith. They may each have had many failures, but none of them failed as I did. My failure was fatal. I killed faith and tore the star of hope out of the black night, leaving only a gaping wound that will never heal.

And I have come to you through that tear in the fabric of despair, to touch your life again with healing grace and divine love.

But surely there are limits, even to God's grace! And I, of all persons, have passed beyond that limit. My name will be remembered without pity. My act of betrayal is my epitaph. No one weeps for me.

You were angry at me, Judas, for reminding you of your failure. Now you're bitter because no one weeps for you.

It is too painful to hear. You speak of healing and hope as though there were still time. But time has come to an end for me. One act of betrayal, like a drop of blood, has spread through the clear water that was my life, contaminating all. I poured it out on the ground. Never again can it be recovered--and if it could, it would be tainted with the blood of betrayal.

You feel sadness for what might have been, and

despair over the irretrievable loss of your life.

Yes, of course! I loved my life and found joy in being your disciple. I really only came alive when you called me to follow you. But I see now that I ran ahead of you and tried to force you into following me!

I have had that temptation myself with respect to my Father. It is not easy to follow when your own desires are not those of your master.

But you did remain faithful, even when others denied you. In the end, you gained your life. In the end, I lost mine. Does not life teach us that what counts is how we die, not how we live?

What counts, Judas, is not our foolish choices, but my Father's gracious calling. My choosing of you counts more than your betrayal of me.

I tried to deny the feelings of love I have for you. That's why my betrayal of you hurts so much. But our relationship can never be the same again.

We can never return to our innocence. The love that has suffered loss is not a crippled love; it can be healed and made a stronger love.

You speak as though we have only had a lover's quarrel! I went beyond denial and even unfaithfulness.

I burned the bridge that made our relationship possible. I cut the cord that bound my heart to yours and my hand to heaven. There is no way back.

That is true. There never was a way back. There is only a way forward. The past can only be returned to us out of the future. Love is greater than faith and hope, because it can heal faithlessness and cure hopelessness.

In a way that I don't understand, you place my act of betrayal and even death by my own hand between us as something that can be forgiven. You have awakened in me the memory of love, but not yet the possibility of its renewal.

To know that you did love me is sufficient to understand that I still love you.

But we have not spoken of the consequence of my action upon your life. My betrayal placed you on the cross just as surely as if I had driven in the nails with my own hands. Not even love can alter the fact that I caused your death.

My destiny was to do the will of the Father, and I was obedient--even to the point of death upon the cross. Your betrayal did not put me there. You can't take away from me what is truly mine!

I will always be remembered as the one who

betrayed you. I had no explanation to give, no justification for my action. I regretted it immediately--but regret is a bitter tonic that never cures.

Betrayal is a transaction between two, the betrayer and the betrayed, with both having a certain power in the exchange. Your power, Judas, was to destroy the relation; mine to preserve it.

I tried to deny my love for you and became blind to your love for me. I have felt the power of that love, now that it is too late. If the sun could have stood still, and the hours and minutes slowed to an imperceptible crawl, there might have been time.

Do you think that all we need to redeem oneself is more time?

I speak only of enough time for you to have found me before I took vengeance upon myself by taking my own life. If betrayal is a transaction between two, death is a solitary act. And death by one's own hand is the most solitary of all deaths.

And you think that by taking your own life you sealed your fate and plunged into the realm that God has forsaken? I have been to the God forsaken place, Judas, it was on the cross, not in the black hole in your own soul. One death in a God forsaken way is enough, I have died that death--and behold I am alive!

I thought I could see, but I was blind. Through your eyes I see my life is no longer flat and one-dimensional. The door which I closed has become transparent. I--I see a different Judas on the other side!

It is not enough to use my eyes, Judas. I have touched yours so that you may see yourself, and for yourself, that you are my friend.

I saw my guilt, but not the shame that blinded me and angered me. I confessed my sin of betrayal and threw the money back at their feet. But something in me cowered like a child caught stealing coins from the box for the poor.

You have discovered what many have yet to see, Judas, that each failure is not merely an offense against God, but a loss of dignity and esteem for the self. Long before you met me, you wove a veil of shame to shield your eyes from the sight of that emaciated child.

Even in my betrayal of you, I sought to protect myself from exposure through a too-quick confession, as though I could merely undo a wrong. But I could not keep the shame from burning through and tormenting me to death. In the end, I crept within it and killed the child that could not be healed.

You are that child, Judas, and of such is the Kingdom of God!

References

The quotation from Christopher Fry (cover) is from: <u>Sleep of Prisoners</u>. London: Oxford University Press, 1951, p. 49.

The quotation from Dag Hammarskjold (p. 5) is from: <u>Markings</u>, New York: Knopf, 1966 p. 110.

The quotation from Søren Kierkegaard (p. 16) is from: <u>Sickness Unto Death</u>. London: Oxford University Press, 1941.

The quotation from Taylor Caldwell (p. 17) is from: <u>The Devil's Advocate</u>. New York: Crown Publishing, 1952, p. 320.

The quotation from Phyllis McGinley (p. 21) is from: <u>Saint-watching</u>. New York: Viking Press, 1969.

The quotation from Søren Kierkegaard (p. 32) is from: <u>Either/Or</u>. New York: Anchor Books, 1959, Frontispiece.

The quotation from Andrew Marvell (p. 33) is from: <u>Andrew Marvell--Complete Poetry</u>, ed. by George de F. Lord. New York: Modern Library, 1968.

The quotation from K. Gibran (p. 68) is from: <u>The Prophet</u>. New York: Alfred Knopf, 1962.

The quotation from Søren Kierkegaard (p. 91) is from: <u>Journals</u>. New York: Harper Torchbook, 1959.

The quotation from Ann Morrow Lindbergh (p. 96) is from: "Bare Tree," The Unicorn. New York: Pantheon Press, 1956, p. 86.

The quotation from Francis Thompson (p. 147) is from: "The Kingdom of Heaven," Selected Poems of Francis Thompson. London: Burns and Oates, 1907, pp. 132-133.

The reference to G. J. Hamann (p. 157) is from: "J. G. Hamann and the Princess Gallitrzi," Philomathes, Robert Palmer and Robert Hamerton-Kelley (eds). The Hague: Martinus Nijhoff, 1971, p. 339.

The reference to Michael Polanyi (p. 161) is from: Personal Knowledge. London: Routledge and Kegan Paul, 1958, p. 322.

The reference to Giordano Bruno in Dietrich Bonhoeffer (p. 169) is from: Letters and Papers From Prison. New York: Macmillan, 1971, p. 375.

The reference to telling the truth in Dietrich Bonhoeffer (173) is from: Ethics. New York: Macmillan, 1955, pp. 64-65.

The reference to Heidegger (p.175) is from: On the Way to Language, Martin Heidegger. New York: Harper and Row, 1971. p. 124.

The dialogue between Jesus and Judas has been adapted from: The Gospel According to Judas--Is There a Limit to God's Forgiveness? Ray S. Anderson. Colorado Springs: NavPress, 1995,

www.ingramcontent.com/pod-product-compliance
Lightning Source LLC
Chambersburg PA
CBHW062000220426
43662CB00011B/1761